A YEAR of FRIDAYS

A YEAR of FRIDAYS

Meditations on Christ Crucified

Beda Brooks

Kevin Mayhew

First published in 1993 by
KEVIN MAYHEW LTD
Rattlesden
Bury St Edmunds
Suffolk IP30 0SZ

ISBN   0 86209 476 3

Front cover: *Lamentation of the Dead Christ*
by Sister Plautilla Nelli (16c).
Reproduced by kind permission of Museo di San Marco
Dell'Angelico, Florence/Bridgeman Art Library, London.

Cover design by Graham Johnstone
Typesetting and Page Creation by Anne Haskell
Printed and bound in Great Britain.

CONTENTS

PREFACE

In the beginning was the Word, and the Word was with God, and the Word was God; . . . And the Word became flesh and dwelt among us, full of grace and truth; . . . And from his fullness have we all received, grace upon grace.' (John 1:1,14,16)

In the fifty two meditations of this book the quest is for the Word whom we first meet in a phrase or sentence from a Gospel on the Passion and Death of Jesus. There follows an encounter through selected verses from the psalms; these are designed to be pondered in depth and prayed as the prayer of Christ Crucified. It has indeed been well said that the only answer to the pain and agony in today's world is the prayer of Christ.

A 'Meditation' links the psalm verses with our own personal lives and the issues which surround us in the modern world, while silent prayer is also encouraged. Finally we recall and cling with the glue of trust to the fact that the victory has already been won by our Redeemer; the Bible provides us with verses which reinforce our hope in the Word.

These meditations have especial relevance on Fridays throughout the year for it is good each week to recall that we were ransomed 'not with perishable things such as silver or gold, but with the precious blood of Christ, like that of a lamb without spot or blemish' (1 Peter 1:18-19). In this way our spiritual understanding of the wondrous salvation mystery is steadily deepened. St Thomas More set Fridays aside as special days of prayer, and we may be sure that this excellent practice, part of a long established Christian tradition, made no insignificant contribution to his development as a person of profound Christian integrity.

At any time of the year these meditations may be a channel of grace and may be repeated again and again so that new insights from the psalms may be discerned. They are helpful both during the Lenten season and on days of recollection. Christian groups, communities and parishes may use them as well as individuals in their own homes or on private retreat.

In particular, it is hoped that this particular selection and arrangement of verses will serve to enhance the capacity for praying the psalms in depth and therefore assist the increasing numbers of those who are now reciting them in the Divine Office and the many who are encountering them in the Sunday and weekday celebration of the Eucharist.

In these pages we may find the crucified Christ and pray through him, with him, in him for ourselves, our Church and our world.

'So, could you not watch with me one hour?' (Matthew 26:40)

INTRODUCTION

After his Resurrection Jesus told the disciples whom he had met on the road to Emmaus that everything written in the psalms about his suffering had to be fulfilled. Guided by these words of the risen Christ, he who is the Way, the Truth, and the Life, we may confidently search for the crucified Christ in the book of the Psalms, aptly described by St Ambrose as one which especially 'breathes the spirit of God's grace'.

Tools to be used in our quest are not only the psalmist's words, sharper than any two-edged sword though they be, but also the silence of our own hearts. The latter constitutes a supremely positive instrument freeing us from so much restlessness so that the .spirit may work in us and the Word resonate through the very depths of our being.

A preliminary consideration of the words of St Augustine, the great early fifth century doctor of the Church, may significantly deepen our praying of the psalmist's verses. He tells us that in the psalms

CHRIST PRAYS FOR US

AND

PRAYS IN US

AND

IS PRAYED TO BY US.

At the appointed hour 'the Word was made flesh and dwelt among us, full of grace and truth' (John 1:14). Assuming the form of a servant, our eternal high priest offered himself on Calvary for the forgiveness of sins and we must recognise that still today *Christ is praying for us as our Priest*. It is our delight to say the psalms

9

through him and *with* him to the Father in the unity of the Holy Spirit, just as we are accustomed to do in the great eucharistic prayers of our liturgy. Our voices are not merely speaking or conforming with his, they are blending or uniting with his, so 'making of the divine and our own will one will only' (St Alphonsus). We are 'a chosen race, a royal priesthood, a holy nation, God's own people' (1 Peter 2:9), set apart to sing the praises of God; we have been called out of darkness into the wonderful light of Christ. We are to be like living stones 'built into a spiritual house, to be a holy priesthood, to offer spiritual sacrifices acceptable to God through Jesus Christ' (1 Peter 2:5).

Furthermore, *Christ is praying in us as our Head*. Thanks to the wonder of our baptism 'into Christ' we have 'put on Christ' (Galatians 3:27) and have become 'a new creation' (2 Corinthians 5:17). The grace to live and pray in him is being bestowed upon us and it is our desire to be 'rooted and built up in him' (Colossians 2:6). We may listen in awe as Jesus both warns and inspires us:

> 'I am the vine, you are the branches. He who abides in me, and I in him, he it is that bears much fruit, for apart from me you can do nothing' (John 15:4-5)

It is therefore our joy to recognise his voice *in* us, saying with St Paul: 'I have been crucified with Christ; it is no longer I who live, but Christ who lives in me; and the life I now live in the flesh I live by faith in the Son of God, who loved me and gave himself for me' (Galatians 2:20). It is thus that we pray *in* him and he *in* us.

'Jesus Christ is the same yesterday and today and for ever' (Hebrews 13:8). And who was he yesterday? 'In the beginning was the Word and the Word was with God, and the Word was God' (John 1:1). Indeed, the Word is God and so in the psalmist's verses *we are praying to Christ as our God*, one God with the Father

10

and the Holy Spirit. We are his creatures: 'Beloved, we are God's children' (1 John 3:2), made in his image and likeness, that is in that of Jesus Christ.

St Ambrose's discourse on the psalms tells us that we shall read in the psalms of Christ's 'great love' 'in submitting to great dangers in order to wipe out the shame of a whole people'; 'in this triumph of virtue we may recognise the great things of which love is capable'. This 'great love' invites our response; and we may go forward with total trust that Christ truly longs to redeem each one of our days and our entire lives. Additional inspiration may be drawn from the fact that the psalms were the very prayers Jesus prayed throughout his life and it is not surprising to find him quoting them while nailed to the cross.

So encouraged let us begin our search for and our meditation on Christ Crucified, remembering that this entails loving his will for us.

'What others have announced in enigmas seems to have been promised quite openly to the psalmist alone . . . This prophet alone announced what no other had dared to say, and what was later preached in the gospel by the Lord himself' (St Ambrose).

PUBLISHER'S NOTE

The Psalms in this book are numbered according to the
Greek Septuagint version and will normally differ from
the Hebrew text by one number, as follows:

Greek Septuagint	Hebrew
1-8	1-8
9	9-10
10-112	11-113
113	114-115
114-115	116
116-145	117-146
146-147	147
148-150	148-150

The numbering of the verses also differs slightly as the
title is incorporated into the body of the Psalm.

Jesus knelt down and prayed

THE WORD IN THE GOSPEL   Luke 22:39,41

Jesus went as was his custom to the Mount of Olives;
and the disciples followed him. And he withdrew from
them about a stone's throw, and knelt down and
prayed.

THE WORD IN THE PSALMS

O that I had wings like a dove   54:7-10
    to fly away and be at rest.
So I would escape far away
    and take refuge in the desert.
I would hasten to find a shelter
    from the raging wind,
    from the destructive storm, O Lord,
    and from their plotting tongues.
Though the wicked lie in wait to destroy me   118:95
    yet I ponder on your will.

To you, O Lord, I call,   27:1
    my rock, hear me.
If you do not heed I shall become
    like those in the grave.
Lord, make haste and answer;   142:7
    for my spirit fails within me.
Do not hide your face
    lest I become like those in the grave.

Let my prayer arise before you like incense,   140:2
    the raising of my hands like an evening oblation.

My help shall come from the Lord   120:2-5
    who made heaven and earth.
Let him sleep not, your guard.

No, he sleeps not nor slumbers,
    Israel's guard.
The Lord is your guard and your shade;
    at your right hand side he stands.
By day the sun shall not smite you   120:6
    nor the moon in the night.

SILENT PRAYER

> Listen to the Lord with the ear of your heart.
> Guard and deliver us from evil.

MEDITATION

The gospels tell us that Jesus prayed in the garden; as a Jew, the prayers he knew so well were the psalms. At all times the phrases of the psalmist flowed naturally from his lips to mingle with his everyday language.

May the psalms be an 'alive and active' dimension of our own prayer.

Help us, Lord God, to find our crucified Saviour in the psalms. May we offer our very selves and may our offering arise before you like incense.

SILENT PRAYER

> Pure prayer rises like fragrant incense
> from a faithful heart.
> Adore the Lord who is teaching us how to pray.

THE WORD OF HOPE   REV 8:3-4

Another angel came and stood at the altar with a golden censer; and he was given much incense to mingle with the prayers of all the saints upon the golden altar before the throne; and the smoke of the incense rose with the prayers of the saints from the hand of the angel before God.

'Not my will,
but yours be done'

THE WORD IN THE GOSPEL   Luke 22:42

'Father, if you are willing, remove this cup from me;
nevertheless not my will, but yours be done'.

THE WORD IN THE PSALMS

You made the moon to mark the months;   103:19,20
> the sun knows the time for its setting.
When you spread the darkness it is night.

Teach me to do your will   142:10-12
> for you, O Lord, are my God.
Let your good spirit guide me
> in ways that are level and smooth.
For your name's sake, Lord, save my life;
> in your justice save my soul from distress.
In your love make an end of my foes;
> destroy all those who oppress me
> for I am your servant, O Lord.
In the morning let me know your love   142:8
> for I put my trust in you.
Make me know the way I should walk:
> to you I lift up my soul.

The Lord has sworn an oath he will not change.   109:4
> 'You are a priest for ever,
> a priest like Melchizedek of old.'

O Lord, it is you who are my portion and cup;   15:5,7
> it is you yourself who are my prize.
I will bless the Lord who gives me counsel,
> who even at night directs my heart.

Silent Prayer

Guide me along the right path.
Increase my trust in your will.

Meditation

In this darkness Jesus shows us that he is truly man. Anticipating his sufferings as the Lamb to be sacrificed in the new covenant, he did not rejoice. We therefore, need not be anxious about our own shrinking from suffering, but rather be strengthened by recognising that it is his will to bestow on us a share in his divine nature.

Grant, Lord, that we may renounce love of self and thereby love ourselves more truly.

May we be wise and prefer your will to what is self-chosen.

Father, not my will, but yours be done.

Silent Prayer

Seek his will this very day.
The cup he offers is a gift of divine love.

The Word Of Hope   Col 1:9b-10

We have not ceased to pray for you, asking that you may be filled with the knowledge of his will in all spiritual wisdom and understanding, to lead a life worthy of the Lord, fully pleasing to him, bearing fruit in every good work and increasing in the knowledge of God.

An angel strengthened him

THE WORD IN THE GOSPEL   Luke 22:43

And there appeared to him an angel from heaven,
    strengthening him.

THE WORD IN THE PSALMS

Lord, answer, for your love is kind;   68:17
    in your compassion, turn towards me.
. . . see the enemy scoffing;   73:18-19
    a senseless people insults your name.
Do not give Israel, your dove, to the hawk.
O Lord, plead my cause against my foes;   34:1,4-6
    fight those who fight me.
Let those who plan evil against me
    be routed in confusion.
Let them be like chaff before the wind;
    let God's angel scatter them.
Let their path be slippery and dark;
    let God's angel pursue them.
You will guide me by your counsel   72:24
    and so you will lead me to glory.

The angel of the Lord is encamped   33:8
    around those who revere him, to rescue them.

Blessed be the Lord, my rock   143:1,2
    who trains my arms for battle,
    who prepares my hands for war.
He is my love, my fortress;
    he is my stronghold, my saviour,
    my shield, my place of refuge.

SILENT PRAYER

> Seek the face of the Lord.
> God's angels strengthen his faithful followers.

MEDITATION

Encircling hawks, the pressures of our society, may threaten to rob us of our very selves with our potential for true development. There are always choices to be made; there is always a loving Father to bestow grace. It was the same for Jesus. Let us pray that we and those who suffer today may retain spiritual freedom and dignity; let us not be puppets of circumstance.

Lord, help us to heal others with the ointment of encouragement and the medicine of divine Scripture.

May we not stifle the spiritual gift within us.

SILENT PRAYER

> We have been called to be like angels of light.
> Dwell in the Lord's presence.

THE WORD OF HOPE   Ex 23:20-21

Behold, I send an angel before you, to guard you on the way and to bring you to the place which I have prepared. Give heed to him and hearken to his voice.

He prayed more earnestly

THE WORD IN THE GOSPEL   Luke 22:44a

And being in an agony he prayed more earnestly.

THE WORD IN THE PSALMS

When I see the heavens, the work of your hands,   8:4,5
    the moon and the stars which you arranged,
what is man that you should keep him in mind,
    mortal man that you care for him,
      man, who is merely a breath   143:4
      whose life fades like a shadow?

O God listen to my prayer,   54:2,3
    do not hide from my pleading,
attend to me and reply;
    with my cares, I cannot rest.
Rescue me, Lord, from evil men;   139:2-5
    from the violent keep me safe,
from those who plan evil in their hearts
    and stir up strife every day;
who sharpen their tongue like an adder's,
    with the poison of viper on their lips.
Lord, guard me from the hands of the wicked;
    from the violent keep me safe;
    they plan to make me stumble.

The Lord is my light and my help;   26:1
    whom shall I fear?
The Lord is the stronghold of my life;
    before whom shall I shrink?

SILENT PRAYER

    Respond whole-heartedly to the light sent by the Lord.
    Enter the inner sanctuary of your soul.

MEDITATION

Jesus assumed our fragile humanity which cried out for the healing of its age-old wounds. From his own experience as man he understands that we are weak and that the way which leads to life is narrow and hard for us.

Let us not be afraid. What is not possible to us by nature the Lord will supply by the help of his grace if we do but ask.

Christ Jesus, grant that we may often devote ourselves to prayer. May we plunge into the depths and search for your will.

Lord, I know that you do care for me and that you are my light and my help.

SILENT PRAYER

Seek the grace for which your soul is yearning.
Resolve to give yourself often to prayer.

THE WORD OF HOPE   Rom 8:26-27

The Spirit helps us in our weakness; for we do not know how to pray as we ought, but the Spirit himself intercedes for us with sighs too deep for words. And he who searches the hearts of men knows what is the mind of the Spirit, because the Spirit intercedes for the saints according to the will of God.

His sweat became
like great drops of blood

THE WORD IN THE GOSPEL   Luke 22:44b

And his sweat became like great drops of blood
    falling down upon the ground.

THE WORD IN THE PSALMS

My soul lies in the dust;   118:25,28
    by your word revive me,
    by your word raise me up.

My heart is stricken within me,   54:5,6
    death's terror is on me,
trembling and fear fall upon me
    and horror overwhelms me.

When my strength fails do not forsake me.   70:9-11
For my enemies are speaking about me;
    those who watch me take counsel together
    saying: 'God has forsaken him; follow him,
    seize him; there is no one to save him.'
Listen, then, to my cry   141:7
    for I am in the depths of distress.
Those who harm me unjustly draw near: 118:150,151
    they are far from your law.
But you, O Lord, are close:
    your commands are truth.

I am sure I shall see the Lord's goodness   26:13,14
    in the land of the living.
Hope in him, hold firm and take heart.
Hope in the Lord!

SILENT PRAYER

The Lord is always compassionate.
He forgives whatever torments our consciences.

MEDITATION

Earlier that same evening Jesus had taken the cup of
wine into his hands at the Paschal Supper and said to
his apostles: 'This is the cup of my blood, the blood of
the new and everlasting covenant. It will be shed for
you and for all so that sins may be forgiven.' In the
garden of Gethsemane so great was his compassion for
us that his sweat became like drops of blood.

Cost what it may, let us prove ourselves, Lord Jesus,
by patient endurance and be recognisable as your
disciples through our love for one another.

Let us hope in the Lord!

SILENT PRAYER

Forgive us our trespasses as we forgive those
who trespass against us.
Grant us your abundant grace.

THE WORD OF HOPE   Eph 1:5-8

He destined us in love to be his sons through Jesus
Christ, according to the purpose of his will, to the praise
of his glorious grace which he freely bestowed on us in
the Beloved. In him we have redemption through his
blood, the forgiveness of our trespasses, according to
the riches of his grace which he lavished upon us.

23

He found his disciples sleeping

THE WORD IN THE GOSPEL   Luke 22:45

And when he rose from prayer, he came to the disciples
and found them sleeping for sorrow.

THE WORD IN THE PSALMS

Who will stand up for me against the wicked?   93:16
   Who will defend me from those who do evil?

O Lord, do not leave me alone,   21:20
   my strength, make haste to help me!
Turn to me and have mercy   24:16,17
   for I am lonely and poor.
Relieve the anguish of my heart
   and set me free from my distress.
O Lord, you know all my longing;   37:10
   my groans are not hidden from you.

Preserve my life and rescue me.   24:20,21
   Do not disappoint me, you are my refuge.
May innocence and uprightness protect me:
   for my hope is in you, O Lord.
This is my comfort in sorrow   118:50,57
   that your promise gives me life.
My part, I have resolved, O Lord,
   is to obey your word.

SILENT PRAYER

   Arouse yourself and see that the Lord is good.
   He is redeeming your life from deadly peril.

24

MEDITATION

The winds of change may blow. The morrow's dawn may not bring visible improvement. Christ is alone, desolate.

Awake my soul, console the Lord in his distress. Set the suffering Christ as a seal on your heart. Today he is the one who is in distress, the one in anguish.

Grant, Lord, that we may arise from apathy and intolerance. Let us open our ears to your voice from heaven.

It is high time to respond to the cry of the poor; bestow on us the quality of mercy.

May we be rooted in the strength of your almighty Word and dare to do what is right, what is compassionate.

SILENT PRAYER

When my heart is faint you raise me up.
An eternal reward is promised to those
who fall asleep in righteousness.

THE WORD OF HOPE   1 John 1:8,9

If we say we have no sin, we deceive ourselves, and the truth is not in us. If we confess our sins, he is faithful and just, and will forgive our sins and cleanse us from all unrighteousness.

'Pray that you may not enter into temptation'

THE WORD IN THE GOSPEL   Luke 22:46

He said to them, 'Why do you sleep? Rise and pray that
you may not enter into temptation.'

THE WORD IN THE PSALMS

Blessed be the Lord, God of Israel,   71:18,19
    ever blessed his glorious name.
He gave a command to our fathers   77:5-8
    to make it known to their children
that the next generation might know it,
    children yet to be born.
They too should arise and tell their sons
    that they too should set their hope in God
    and never forget God's deeds
    but keep every one of his commands:
so that they night not be like their fathers,
    a defiant and rebellious race,
    a race whose heart was fickle,
    whose spirit was unfaithful to God.

How often they defied him in the wilderness   77:40,31,37
    and caused him pain in the desert!
God's anger rose against them.
He slew the strongest among them,
    struck down the flower of Israel ,
For their hearts were not truly with him;
    they were not faithful to his covenant.

Love the Lord, all you saints.   30;24,25
    He guards his faithful
    but the Lord will repay to the full
    those who act with pride.

Be strong, let your heart take courage,
　　all who hope in the Lord.

SILENT PRAYER

Lead us not into temptation.
Be neither apathetic and idle nor rebellious and defiant.

MEDITATION

Christ speaks. It is the wise who build their house on
rock. The floods may rise, the hurricanes hammer
against the house, but, founded on the rock of prayer, it
does not fall. Many indeed are the temptations we
encounter and their strength is never to be
underestimated, yet persistent prayer overcomes
temptations, supports the stumbling, guides the
uncertain and raises the fallen.

Lord, grant that we may always remember your
wonderful deeds and be steadfast. May we receive the
inner strength to endure and resist temptations. Let us
accept the challenge of conveying our faith to the next
generation.

SILENT PRAYER

Be persevering in prayer and enter not into temptation.
Never forget the Lord abounds in steadfast love.

THE WORD OF HOPE   Rev 2:10-11

Do not fear what you are about to suffer. Behold, the
devil is about to throw some of you into prison, that you
may be tested, and for ten days you will have
tribulation. Be faithful unto death, and I will give you
the crown of life. He who has an ear, let him hear what
the Spirit says to the churches. He who conquers shall
not be hurt by the second death.

There came a crowd
and Judas was leading them

THE WORD IN THE GOSPEL   Luke 22:47a

While he was still speaking, there came a crowd, and
the man called Judas, one of the twelve, was leading
them.

THE WORD IN THE PSALMS

Here is one who is pregnant with malice,	7:15
conceives evil and brings forth lies.	
Sin speaks to the sinner	35:2,4
in the depths of his heart.	
In his mouth are mischief and deceit.	
All wisdom is gone.	
His speech is softer than butter,	54:22
but war is in his heart.	
His words are smoother than oil,	
but they are naked swords.	

If this had been done by an enemy	54:13-15
I could bear his taunts.	
If a rival had risen against me,	
I could hide from him.	
But it is you, my own companion,	
my intimate friend!	
(How close was the friendship between us)	
We walked together in harmony	
in the house of God.	

Thus even my friend, in whom I trusted,	40:10-11
who ate my bread, has turned against me.	
But you, O Lord, have mercy on me.	

This I know, that God is on my side.	55:10-12

In God, whose word I praise,
(in the Lord, whose word I praise,)
in God I trust; I shall not fear:
what can mortal man do to me?

SILENT PRAYER

Be loyal to Jesus our Saviour
By our fruits we shall be known.

MEDITATION

The one pregnant with malice attracted the crowd; the companion was betraying his intimate friend. Jesus, the man of sorrows, encountered treachery.

We, who once followed blindly along the dark road of death, are now being led by Christ our light along the highway of grace.

Jesus, may my way of acting be different from the world's way. Let me become one in whom there is no guile, one who lives simply, and simply for you.

O Lord, have mercy on me.

SILENT PRAYER

Love those who thwart and resist you.
Do good to those who oppose and annoy you.

THE WORD OF HOPE   1 Thess 5:5,9

You are all sons of light and sons of the day; we are not of the night or of darkness. For God has not destined us for wrath, but to obtain salvation through our Lord Jesus Christ.

Judas drew near to Jesus

THE WORD IN THE GOSPEL   Luke 22:47b

He drew near to Jesus to kiss him.

THE WORD IN THE PSALMS

Why do you boast of your wickedness,   51:3,4
    you champion of evil,
    you master of deceit?

In his pride the wicked says:
    'He will not punish.   9,10:4,5,7-10
    There is no God.' Such are his thoughts.
His path is ever untroubled;
    your judgement is far from his mind.
His mouth is full of cursing, guile, oppression,
    mischief and deceit under his tongue.
His eyes are on the watch for the helpless man.
He lurks in hiding like a lion in his lair;
    he lurks in hiding to seize the poor.
He crouches, preparing to spring,
The deceitful and bloodthirsty man   5:7
    the Lord detests.

Though an army encamp against me   26:3
    my heart would not fear.
Though war break out against me
    even then would I trust.
In God is my safety and glory,   61:8,9
    the rock of my strength.
Take refuge in God all you people.
    Trust him at all times.
Pour out your hearts before him
    for God is our refuge.

30

SILENT PRAYER

Love the Lord your God with all the simplicity of
your heart.

MEDITATION

The man of sorrows is acquainted not only with the
betrayal of Judas, but with our betrayals, deviousness
and cunning. It is said that the just sin seven times a
day. Are we even as good as the just? Yet, never at any
moment is Jesus unfaithful to us.

Father, grant us steadfast faith that we may draw
near to the Word with sincere hearts and embrace the
Good News. May we show no displeasure when we
meet with indifference or ingratitude from those to
whom we have done some kindness. Mary, virgin ever
faithful, intercede for us.

SILENT PRAYER

With loving hearts come close to Jesus.
He will reward his faithful servants.

THE WORD OF HOPE   Jas 4:7-8,10

Submit yourselves therefore to God. Resist the devil
and he will flee from you. Draw near to God and he will
draw near to you. Humble yourselves before the Lord
and he will exalt you.

31

'Would you betray the Son of Man with a kiss?'

THE WORD IN THE GOSPEL   Luke 22:48

Jesus said to him, 'Judas, would you betray the Son of Man with a kiss?'

THE WORD IN THE PSALMS

Lord, who shall dwell on your holy mountain?   14:1,3,5
He who does no wrong to his brother,
    and accepts no bribes against the innocent.
Such a man will stand firm for ever.

The Lord is high yet he looks on the lowly   137:6
    and the haughty he knows from afar.
The wicked man plots against the just   36:12
    and gnashes his teeth against him.
He digs a pitfall, digs it deep;   7:16,17
    and in the trap he has made he will fall.
His malice will recoil on himself;
    on his own head violence will fall.
I have seen the wicked triumphant,   36:35,36,17
    towering like a cedar of Lebanon,
I passed by again; he was gone.
    I searched; he was nowhere to be found
for the power of the wicked shall be broken
    and the Lord will support the just.
From the dust he lifts up the lowly.   112:7

The Lord is my strength and my shield;   27:7,8
    in him my heart trusts.
The Lord is the strength of his people,
    a fortress where his anointed find help.

Silent Prayer

You have been invited and chosen.
Gladly work all the harder.

Meditation

In this garden Jesus was betrayed for the sake of us who left the Garden of Eden. If we embrace with all the power of our souls the One who is the true light, even here and now we may begin dwelling on his holy mountain.

Grant, Lord, that we may acquire the divine art of forgiveness. May we love others with a deeper compassion and understanding. Forgive us our sins of pride and anger; may we be meek and humble of heart.

Silent Prayer

Learn from me for I am meek and humble of heart and you will find rest for your souls.

The Word Of Hope   Phil 2:5-10

Have this mind among yourselves, which was in Christ Jesus, who, though he was in the form of God, did not count equality with God a thing to be grasped, but emptied himself, taking the form of a servant, being born in the likeness of men. And being found in human form he humbled himself and became obedient unto death, even death on a cross. Therefore God has highly exalted him and bestowed on him the name which is above every name, that at the name of Jesus every knee should bow, in heaven and on earth and under the earth.

'Lord, shall we strike with the sword?'

THE WORD IN THE GOSPEL   Luke 22:49-51

And when those who were about him saw what would follow, they said, 'Lord, shall we strike with the sword?' And one of them struck the slave of the high priest and cut off his right ear. But Jesus said, 'No more of this!' And he touched his ear and healed him.

THE WORD IN THE PSALMS

Happy the man who considers the poor
    and the weak.   40:2
      The Lord will save him in the day of evil.

See the just man, mark the upright,   36:37-39
    for the peaceful man a future lies in store,
but sinners shall all be destroyed.
    No future lies in store for the wicked.
The salvation of the just comes from the Lord,
    their stronghold in time of distress.
You search my heart, you visit me by night.   16:3-4
    You test me and you find in me no wrong.
    My words are not sinful as are men's words.
Long enough have I been dwelling   119: 6
    with those who hate peace.

Consider the Lord and his strength;   104:4
    constantly seek his face.
    Seek and strive after peace.   33:15
The Lord will not refuse any good   83:12-13
    to those who walk without blame.
Lord, God of hosts,
    happy the man who trusts in you.

SILENT PRAYER

Behold the Lamb of God who heals the wounds of sin in the world.

Lord, make me an instrument of your peace
and of your healing.

MEDITATION

'Lord, shall we strike with the sword?' Only a sword?
Today, Lord, we ask: 'Shall 'they' strike with an atom, or
a chemical, or a germ? The spectre of nuclear, chemical
and germ warfare visits us 'by night'. Today's science
fiction may become tomorrow's fact. A minute terrorist
cell may hold a city or community to ransom.
Something of the scale of the international arms trade is
revealed to all when conflicts flare, and weapons
become obsolete almost as soon as they are marketed.
We sinners arm ourselves with sarcastic, cynical and
bitter words to hurl with smug self-satisfaction at those
who hurt or threaten us.

Grant us, Lord, your forgiveness. May we not lose
our nerve in the modern world, but keep our eyes fixed
on you. Your prayer is the answer to violence and in this
we share. The psalms are among our noblest weapons
and we need fear no adversary when we have learned
how to wield them. May we see the victory of the Lord
on our behalf.

SILENT PRAYER

All shall see the saving power of our God.
Be compassionate as our Redeemer is compassionate.

THE WORD OF HOPE   Is 32:16-18

Then justice will dwell in the wilderness,
    and righteousness abide in the fruitful field.
And the effect of righteousness will be peace,
    and the result of righteousness,
    quietness and trust for ever.
My people will abide in a peaceful habitation,
    in secure dwellings, and in quiet resting places.

35

They seized Jesus

THE WORD IN THE GOSPEL   cf Luke 22:52,54

The chief priests and captains of the temple and elders
who had come out against Jesus seized him.

THE WORD IN THE PSALMS

My foes encircle me with deadly intent.   16:9-12
    Their hearts tight shut, their mouths
    speak proudly.
They advance against me, and now they
    surround me.
Their eyes are watching to strike me
    to the ground
as though they were lions ready to claw
    or like some young lion crouched in hiding.
They band together in ambush,   55:7
    track me down and seek my life.

Hear the voice of my pleading   27:2,3
    as I call for help,
as I lift up my hands in prayer
    to your holy place.
Do not drag me away with the wicked,
    with the evil doers.
Do not grant the wicked their desire   139:9
    nor let their plots succeed.

So let every good man pray to you   31:6,7
    in time of need.
The floods of water may reach high
    but him they shall not reach.
You are my hiding place, O Lord.
If you uphold me I shall be unharmed   40:13
    and set in your presence for ever more.

SILENT PRAYER

> Release me from the snares they have hidden.
> Jesus, support me with your grace.

MEDITATION

Christ's enemies are active and their action stems from pride and hatred. Today we are living in an unstable hyper-active world.

Lord, help us to learn to be silent and still so that we may hear your Word.

May we allow the Spirit of God to mould our souls so that our actions may flow from our sharing in the divinity of Christ who humbled himself to share in our humanity.

Deepen within us a quiet understanding of those words of a carol:

> He came all so still
> where his mother lay,
> like dew in April
> that falleth on the spray.

SILENT PRAYER

> Free your mind from whatever weighs it down.
> Be still and soar into the heavens.

THE WORD OF HOPE   Luke 11:9,10

And I tell you, ask, and it will be given you; seek, and you will find; knock, and it will be opened to you. For every one who asks receives, and he who seeks finds, and to him who knocks it will be opened.

They led Jesus to the high priest

THE WORD IN THE GOSPEL   Luke 22:54

They led him away, bringing him into the high priest's house.

THE WORD IN THE PSALMS

The wicked man watches for the just   36:32,14
    and seeks occasion to kill him.
The sword of the wicked is drawn,
    his bow is bent to slaughter the upright.
There is no fear of God   35:2
    before his eyes.

Lord, you hear the prayer of the poor;   9,10:17,18
. . . you turn your ear
    so that mortal man may strike terror no more.

Though the proud may utterly deride me   118:51,72,163,76,77
    I keep to your law.
The law from your mouth means more to me
    than silver and gold.
Lies I hate and detest
    but your law is my love.
Let your love be ready to console me
    by your promise to your servant.
Let your love come and I shall live
    for your law is my delight.

SILENT PRAYER

    Offer yourself to be led where the Father wills.
    Equally do not resist the 'when' and 'how' of his will.

MEDITATION

Jesus made no effort to escape, but offered himself to die for us. We have been redeemed by him and made a new creation in the Holy Spirit and the Spirit is to be our rule of life.

Recent human progress has brought with it great temptations; the order of values is confused.

May we be endowed with the wisdom to differentiate between legislation which extinguishes life and strikes terror, and that which nurtures life and upholds Christian standards.

May our mortal legislators cherish and give expression to the life and light of the immortal Word since through him comes grace and truth. Let us always remember that Christ came that we may have life and have it more abundantly.

SILENT PRAYER

I am the light of the world.
Anyone who follows me will have the light of life.

THE WORD OF HOPE   1 Cor 1:23-25

We preach Christ crucified, a stumbling block to Jews and folly to Gentiles, but to those who are called, both Jews and Greeks, Christ the power of God and the wisdom of God. For the foolishness of God is wiser than men, and the weakness of God is stronger than men.

Caiaphas was the high priest that year

THE WORD IN THE GOSPEL cf John 18:13-14

Caiaphas was high priest that year. It was Caiaphas who had given counsel to the Jews that it was expedient that one man should die for the people.

THE WORD IN THE PSALMS

O Lord, how great are your works. 91:6,7
    How deep are your designs!
The foolish man cannot know this
    and the fool cannot understand.

O Lord my God, deliver me! 114:4
Take up your buckler and shield; 34:2,3,7
    arise to help me.
Take up the javelin and the spear
    against those who pursue me.
O Lord, say to my soul:
    'I am your salvation.'
They have hidden a net for me wantonly;
    they have dug a pit.
Turn your eyes, O God, our shield, 83:10
    look on the face of your anointed.
Let the oil of the wicked not anoint my head. 140:5
May your hand be on the man you have chosen, 79:18
    the man you have given your strength.

Great are the works of the Lord; 110:2
    to be pondered by all who love them.

SILENT PRAYER

> Terrible demands may be made by love.
> With his blood he bought us for God.

MEDITATION

How great are God's works and how deep his designs. Jesus, the beloved Son of the Father, was to suffer and die for our sake. In pity he bent down to overcome the world.

Let us offer our very selves in Spirit and in truth for the good of the Church and the world. Grant, Lord, that by prayer-filled lives we may bring new vision to our society and new hope for the future of humanity. May the policies of our rulers in Church and State be shaped by a deep sense of man's immortal destiny.

SILENT PRAYER

> Behold the infinite treasure of Christ.
> Renew your vision of hope in him.

THE WORD OF HOPE   1 John 4:9-11

In this the love of God was made manifest among us, that God sent his only Son into the world, so that we might live through him. In this is love, not that we loved God but that he loved us and sent his Son to be the expiation for our sins. Beloved, if God so loved us, we also ought to love one another.

They sought false testimony against Jesus

THE WORD IN THE GOSPEL   Matt 26:59-60a

Now the chief priests and the whole council sought
false testimony against Jesus that they might put him to
death, but they found none.

THE WORD IN THE PSALMS

False witnesses rise against me   26:12
    breathing out fury.
They sharpen their tongues likes swords;   63:4-6
    they aim bitter words like arrows
to shoot at the innocent from ambush,
    shooting suddenly and recklessly.
They scheme their evil course;
    they conspire to lay secret snares.

To the Lord in the hour of my distress   119:1
    I call and he answers me,
Reach down from heaven and save me;   143:7,8
    draw me out from the mighty waters,
from the hands of alien foes
    whose mouths are filled with lies,
    whose hands are raised in perjury.
Do not let my lying foes   34:19-20
    rejoice over me.
Do not let those who hate me unjustly
    wink eyes at each other.
They wish no peace to the peaceful
    who live in the land.

I will hear what the Lord God has to say,   84:9,10
    a voice that speaks of peace,

peace for his people and his friends
and those who turn to him in their hearts.
His help is near for those who fear him
and his glory will dwell in our land.

SILENT PRAYER

Seek the eternal values expressed in the person of Jesus.
Be a channel of the Lord's peace to his people.

MEDITATION

The voices of false witnesses do not speak of peace for
the people. If we wish to bear witness to the Truth our
lives must not be adapted to the pattern of this present
world. If we wish to please God we must expect to pass
through many trials.

Let us not forget that, being in the communion of
saints, we are surrounded by a great cloud of witnesses.

May we guard against spiritual blindness and
ingrained prejudice inherited from previous
generations.

Grant us, Lord, the courage to bear true testimony in
times of crisis and not to count the cost.

SILENT PRAYER

Refute falsehood and do so with gentleness,
Fill spirit, soul and body with the truth of Christ.

THE WORD OF HOPE   Phil 4:8,9b

Brethren, whatever is true, whatever is honourable,
whatever is just, whatever is pure, whatever is lovely,
whatever is gracious, if there is any excellence, if there is
anything worthy of praise, think about these things.
And the God of peace will be with you.

False witnesses

cf Matt 26: 60

THE WORD IN THE GOSPEL

Many false witnesses came forward.

THE WORD IN THE PSALMS

Lying witnesses arise   34:11,12,17
    and accuse me unjustly.
They repay me evil for good:
    my soul is forlorn.
O Lord, how long will you look on?
    Come to my rescue!
Save my life from these raging beasts,
    my soul from these lions.
Help, O Lord, for good men have vanished: 11:2,3
    truth has gone from the sons of men.
Falsehood they speak one to another,
    with lying lips, with a false heart.

May the Lord destroy all lying lips,   11:4,5
    the tongue that speaks high-sounding words,
those who say: 'Our tongue is our strength;
    our lips are our own, who is our master?'
They scheme their evil course;   63:6,7
    they conspire to lay secret snares.
They say: 'Who will see us?
    Who can search out our crimes?'
He will search who searches the mind   63:7
    and knows the depths of the heart.

But the king shall rejoice in God,   62:12
    (all that swear by him shall be blessed)
for the mouth of liars shall be silenced.

Silent Prayer

> You are the light of the world.
> Your light must shine in the sight of others.

Meditation

If we are to come forward as true witnesses, we must ensure that our vision of Christ becomes ever clearer. It is when the vision grows dim that tragedies happen. Let us never forget the truth of Christ's redeeming love. Our young people are vulnerable to the onslaught of distorted images flowing from the mass media, but they have the potential to receive, live and spread the Good News.

Lord, may our teenagers acquire the art of discerning which of the many voices they hear are in tune with truth and justice. May we be the Word's true witnesses.

Silent Prayer

> Love your neighbour.
> Whoever is angry with another will answer for it
> before the court.

The Word Of Hope   Mic 6:8

He has showed you, O man, what is good;
and what does the Lord require of you
but to do justice, and to love kindness,
and to walk humbly with your God?

Have you no answer to make?

THE WORD IN THE GOSPEL   Matt 26: 60b-62a

At last two came forward, and said, 'This fellow said,
"I am able to destroy the temple of God, and to build it
in three days".' And the High priest stood up and said,
'Have you no answer to make?'

THE WORD IN THE PSALMS

Who shall climb the mountain of the Lord?   23:3,4
     Who shall stand in his holy place?
The man with clean hands and pure heart,
     who desires not worthless things.

Those who plot against my life lay snares;   37:13-15
those who speak of ruin speak of harm,
     planning treachery all the day long.
But I am like the deaf who cannot hear,
     Like the dumb unable to speak.
I am like a man who hears nothing,
     in whose mouth is no defence.

Set, O Lord, a guard over my mouth;   140:3
     keep watch, O Lord, at the door of my lips!
O God whom I praise, do not be silent: 108:1,2
     for the mouths of deceit and wickedness
     are opened against me.
O Lord, you have seen, do not be silent,   34:22
     do not stand afar off!
I count on you, O Lord;   37:16
     it is you, Lord God, who will answer.

Entrust your cares to the Lord   54:23
     and he will support you.
He will never allow
     the just man to stumble.

Silent Prayer

Proclaim the Good News by the way you live.
I shall put my spirit in you.

Meditation

We too face challenging situations. On occasion we may agonise: should we or should we not speak? Should we speak at length or briefly, with strong emphasis or in gentle tones? May we remember that the wisdom which comes from Jesus is characterised by its purity and peacefulness. Grant us Lord, the grace to respond as you would wish in every testing circumstance.

It is Christ who suffers in all, enduring adversity for the sake of what is true, noble and right. Let us intercede for those facing threatening interrogation and being tested like gold in the furnace. O Lord, bestow on them your sustaining grace.

Silent Prayer

Peacemakers are the sons of God.
My tongue shall proclaim your peace.

The Word Of Hope   Col 3:15

Let the peace of Christ rule in your hearts, to which indeed you were called in the one body. And be thankful.

Jesus was silent

The Word In The Gospel
THE WORD IN THE GOSPEL   Matt 26: 63a

But Jesus was silent.

THE WORD IN THE PSALMS

I said: '. . .   38:2-3,5-6,8,10
   I will put a curb on my lips
   when the wicked man stands before me.'
I was dumb, silent and still.
'O Lord, you have shown me my end,
   how short is the length of my days.
Now I know how fleeting is my life.
   You have given me a short span of days.'
And now, Lord, what is there to wait for?
   In you rests all my hope.
I was silent, not opening my lips,
   because this was all your doing.

For your name's sake act in my defence;   108:21
   in the goodness of your love be my rescuer.
Rescue me, God, from my foes;   58: 2-3
   protect me from those who attack me.
O rescue me from those who do evil
   and save me from bloodthirsty men.

Let there be joy for those who love my cause,   34:27,28
   Let them say without end:
   'Great is the Lord who delights
   in the peace of his servant.'
Then my tongue shall speak of your justice,
   all day long of your praise.

SILENT PRAYER

> Ponder the silences of Jesus and thus grow to
> spiritual maturity.
> His words have the dynamism of deeds and his
> silence the significance of speech.

MEDITATION

When we are under real pressure or attack we can
easily become discouraged; we sense or feel the
hostility in the heart of another. Our need is for greater
inner strength, a sense of what really constitutes reality.
This strength for the struggle with evil in ourselves and
in the world we can find only in Jesus. We need an
inner silence, the deep tranquillity of our spiritual life,
and this must be cultivated over many years. Brooding
over past injustices with forgiveness far from our hearts
is nothing but a noisy cul-de-sac.

Lord, may we live disciplined lives of love. Grant us
the grace to ponder quietly, absorbing the signs of our
times and interpreting them in the light of timeless
Christian values.

SILENT PRAYER

> Discern when to speak and when to be silent.
> Seek integrity and look to the Lord in his strength.

THE WORD OF HOPE   Prov 3:13-15

Happy is the man who finds wisdom,
    and the man who gets understanding,
for the gain from it is better than the gain from silver
    and its profit better than gold.
She is more precious than jewels,
    and nothing you desire can compare with her.

49

The high priest said, 'He has uttered blasphemy'

THE WORD IN THE GOSPEL   Matt 26:63-65a

And the high priest said to him, 'I adjure you by the living God, tell us if you are the Christ, the Son of God.' Jesus said to him, 'You have said so. But I tell you, hereafter you will see the Son of man seated at the right hand of Power, and coming on the clouds of heaven." Then the high priest tore his robes and said, 'He has uttered blasphemy.'

THE WORD IN THE PSALMS

Give judgement for me, Lord; I am just   7:9,7
    and innocent of heart.
Lord, rise up in your anger,
    rise against the fury of my foes;
my God, awake! You will give judgement.

My foes crush me all day long,   55:3,6
    for many fight proudly against me.
All day long they distort my words,
    all their thought is to harm me.
Thus your enemies taunt me, O Lord,   88:52
    mocking your anointed at every step.

See, they lie in wait for my life;   58:4,5
    powerful men band together against me.
For no offence, no sin of mine, Lord,
    for no guilt of mine they rush to take their stand.
They speak to me with lying tongues;   108:3,5
    they beset me with words of hate
    and attack me without cause.
They repay me evil for good,
    hatred for love.
Awake, come to my aid and see!   58:5

Let men know that God is the ruler   58:14
  over Jacob and the ends of the earth.

SILENT PRAYER

The state of Jesus was divine.
Let his glorious message dwell within you.

MEDITATION

We believe that you, Lord Jesus, are the Christ, the Son of the Living God. May we prefer nothing to the love of you.

This involves working out our sense of priorities in life and recognising the false gods in our society since these may undermine our worship of the almighty and eternal Lord. The power of the true God is always at work and he is generous with his help. Let us appreciate that he who is the Mighty One is doing great things for us and holy is his name. Even through our powerlessness he is operating. May we be open to his grace.

SILENT PRAYER

He is our Emmanuel, 'God-is-with-us'.
Glory be to the Father, and to the Son,
and to the Holy Spirit.

THE WORD OF HOPE   2 Cor 6:16

What agreement has the temple of God with idols?
For we are the temple of the living God; as God said,
  'I will live in them and move among them,
  and I will be their God,
  and they shall be my people.'

'He deserves death'

THE WORD IN THE GOSPEL   Matt 26: 65a, 66

. . . The high priest said 'What is your judgement?'
They answered, 'He deserves death.'

THE WORD IN THE PSALMS

He, the Lord, is our God: 104:7
    his judgements prevail in all the earth.
O that today you would listen to his voice!   94:7

'Harden not your hearts as at Meribah,   94:8-11
    as on that day at Massah in the desert
when your fathers put me to the test;
    when they tried me, though they saw my work.
For forty years; I was wearied of these people
    and I said: "Their hearts; are astray,
    these people do not know my ways."
Then I took an oath in my anger:
    "Never shall they enter my rest".'

I have heard the slander of the crowd,   30:14
    fear is all around me,
as they plot together against me,
    as they plan to take my life.
'What profit would my death be, my going to
    the grave?   29:10
    Can dust give you praise or proclaim
    your truth?'
Lord God, I take refuge in you.   7:2,3
    From my pursuer save me and rescue me,
lest he tear me to pieces like a lion
    and drag me off with no one to rescue me.

When the wicked are judged they shall not stand,   1:5,6
    nor find room among those who are just;

for the Lord guards the way of the just
    but the way of the wicked leads to doom.
Make justice your sacrifice and trust in the Lord.   4:6

SILENT PRAYER

I will remove the heart of stone from their bodies and
give them a heart of flesh instead.

MEDITATION

O that today we would listen to the voice of Christ as he
speaks to us in the sufferings of so many nations,
communities and families. May our opinions and
assessments be formed in conformity with him. Once
we do hear, may we respond and not look back.

    He will continue speaking through the circumstances
of our lives. May we live not for ourselves but for him,
doing our best, hour by hour, with whatever he chooses
to give us. Then he can surely use us. Let us not be
deafened by our own narrow condemnatory
judgements.

SILENT PRAYER

    If we renounce all our sins we will certainly live.
    Repent and live.

THE WORD OF HOPE   Is 55:3

Incline your ear, and come to me;
    hear, that your soul may live;
and I will make with you an everlasting covenant,
    my steadfast, sure love for David.

53

They spat in his face

Then they spat in his face, and struck him.

THE WORD IN THE PSALMS

All day long my disgrace is before me: 43:16,17,24,25
     my face is covered with shame
at the voice of the taunter, the scoffer,
     at the sight of the foe and avenger.
Awake, O Lord, why do you sleep?
     Why do you hide your face?
O Lord, hear my voice when I call;   26: 7,8
     have mercy and answer.
Of you my heart has spoken:
     'Seek his face.'
     It is your face, O Lord, that I seek.

Do not abandon or forsake me,   26:9
     O God my help!
Lord, I am deeply afflicted: 118:107,22
     by your word give me life.
Relieve me from scorn and contempt
     for I do your will .
Give heed, O Lord, to my prayer   85:6,7
     and attend to the sound of my voice.
In the day of distress I will call
     and surely you will reply.

You who fear the Lord give him praise;   21:24,25
     all sons of Jacob, give him glory,
Revere him, Israel's sons.
     For he has never despised
     nor scorned the poverty of the poor.
From him he has not hidden his face,
     but he heard the poor man when he cried.

SILENT PRAYER

> Ponder the example Christ left us.
> Follow in his footsteps.

MEDITATION

It was for us that Christ suffered these insults. He endured the spittle on his face that the life once wondrously breathed into us could be still more wondrously restored to us. When we are hurt by those who taunt and ridicule us, may we forgive immediately and truly seek his face. We are not to brood over injuries and retreat from the Christian vanguard.

Grant us, Lord, the grace to seek your face with all our strength and all your grace.

Let us also pray for those ethnic groups who for centuries have never known peace, but have experienced uprisings and massacres, torture and violent death.

SILENT PRAYER

> Come back to me with all your heart.
> The Lord is all tenderness and will protect you.

THE WORD OF HOPE   1 Pet 3:13-15a

Now who is there to harm you if you are zealous for what is right? But even if you do suffer for righteousness' sake, you will be blessed. Have no fear of them, nor be troubled but in your hearts reverence Christ as Lord.

They took counsel against Jesus

THE WORD IN THE GOSPEL   Matt 27:1-2a

When morning came, all the chief priests and elders of the people took counsel against Jesus to put him to death, and they bound him.

THE WORD IN THE PSALMS

I can see nothing but violence   54:10-12
   and strife in the city.
Night and day they patrol
   high on the city walls.
It is full of wickedness and evil;
   it is full of sin.
Its streets are never free
   from tyranny and deceit.
The proud have hidden a trap,   139:6
   have spread out lines in a net,
   set snares across my path.

My soul lies down among lions,   56:5
   who would devour the sons of men.
Their teeth are spears and arrows,
   their tongue a sharpened sword.
My wanton enemies are numberless   37:20
   and my lying foes are many.
In return for my love they accuse me   108:4
   while I pray for them.

How great is the goodness, Lord,   30:20-22
   that you keep for those who fear you,
   that you show to those who trust you
   in the sight of man.
You hide them in the shelter of your presence
   from the plotting of men:
   you keep them safe within your tent
   from disputing tongues.

Blessed be the Lord who has shown me
   the wonder of his love
   in a fortified city.

SILENT PRAYER

My people will abide in peaceful habitations,
in secure dwellings, and in quiet resting places.

MEDITATION

Violence and strife are still with us in cities throughout
the modern world. Political, economic and social
problems abound. Those intent on financial gain often
target young people as their potential market. Jesus and
all he stands for may be ignored or counsel taken
against him.

May we come in faith and love to the great King's
city, the place where Jesus dwells. Let our deliberations
be centred on Christ and not on lesser matters.

May we come to appreciate that when we discuss
justice or peace or truth Christ is our subject and our
inspiration.

SILENT PRAYER

The world as we know it is changing.
The Son of man is coming at an hour you do not expect.

THE WORD OF HOPE   Rev 21:1-2,22

Then I saw a new heaven and a new earth; for the first
heaven and the first earth had passed away, and the sea
was no more. And I saw the holy city, new Jerusalem,
coming down out of heaven from God, prepared as a
bride adorned for her husband. And I saw no temple in
the city, for its temple is the Lord God the Almighty and
the Lamb.

'What accusation do you bring against this man?'

The Word In The Psalms   John 18:28a,29

Then they led Jesus from the house of Caiaphas to the praetorium. It was early . . . Pilate went out to meet them and said, 'What accusation do you bring against this man?'

The Word In The Psalms

Call on me in the day of distress   49:15
   I will free you and you shall honour me.

To my words give ear, O Lord,   5:2-4
   give heed to my groaning.
Attend to the sound of my cries,
   my King and my God.
It is you whom I invoke, O Lord.
   In the morning you hear me;
in the morning I offer you my prayer,
   watching and waiting.
Give judgement for me, O Lord,   25:1,3,9-11
   for I walk the path of perfection
   and I walk according to your truth.
Do not sweep me away with sinners,
   nor my life with bloodthirsty men
in whose hands are evil plots.
I walk the path of perfection.

It is time for the Lord to act   118:126
   for your law has been broken.
But you, O Lord, will endure for ever   101:13-14
   and your name from age to age.
You will arise and have mercy on Zion;
   for this is the time to have mercy,
   (yes, the time appointed has come).

Silent Prayer

> Live in my sight and be perfect.
> Be faithful even in small things.

Meditation

What accusation do you bring against this man who had gone about doing good? Let us recognise him as the one who is still doing good and is loving each one of us with a love that is personal and real. He bore our sins and prayed constantly for sinners. So, what can separate us from the love of Christ? When or where could we be separated?

May we lay down our lives for others just as he laid down his life for us.

Let us walk in the path of perfection, strengthened each day by our morning offering and prayer.

Lord, we intercede for all those for whom this very day is a day of distress.

Silent Prayer

> Love one another more sincerely.
> Recall how deeply Christ has loved us.

The Word Of Hope   Rom 8:35,37-39

Who shall separate us from the love of Christ? Shall tribulation, or distress, or persecution, or famine, or nakedness, or peril, or sword?

No, in all these things we are more than conquerors through him who loved us. For I am sure that neither death, nor life, nor angels, nor principalities, nor things present, nor things to come, nor powers, nor height, nor depth, nor anything else in all creation, will be able to separate us from the love of God in Christ Jesus our Lord.

'My Kingship is not of this world'

THE WORD IN THE GOSPEL   John 18:33,36a

Pilate entered the praetorium again and called Jesus,
and said to him, 'Are you the King of the Jews?' . . .
Jesus answered, 'My kingship is not of this world'.

THE WORD IN THE PSALMS

Why this tumult among nations,   2:1,2
    among peoples this useless murmuring?
They arise, the kings of the earth,
    princes plot against the Lord and his Anointed.

The Lord is king; . . .   98:1
    he is throned on the cherubim.
The Lord is great and worthy to be praised   47:2-4,13-15
    in the city of our God.
His holy mountain rises in beauty,
    the joy of all the earth,
    the Great King's city!
God in the midst of its citadels,
    has shown himself its stronghold.
Walk through Zion, walk all round it;
    count the number of its towers.
Review all its ramparts,
examine its castles,
    that you may tell the next generation
that such is our God,
    our God for ever and always.
It is he who leads us.

O Lord, arise in your strength.   20:14
Age to age shall proclaim your works,   144:4,7,13
    shall declare your mighty deeds;
    age to age shall ring out your justice.
Yours is an everlasting kingdom;
    your rule lasts from age to age.

SILENT PRAYER

May your kingdom come.
Yours is an everlasting realm of peace.

MEDITATION

The kingdom not of this world is within everyone who has been reborn in Christ. Let our primary quest be for the kingdom of God and his justice. Earthly rulers find their sovereignty in military power and economic strength; Christ Jesus founded his sovereignty in the insults of the cross.

May we who have been baptised into his saving death live as people who are not of this world. Let us not be involved in useless murmuring, but in seeking God's glory.

Grant us, Lord, protection from the evil one. Bestow blessings on the Church, the Great King's city.

SILENT PRAYER

I leave you peace.
Look not on our sins, but on the faith of your Church.

THE WORD OF HOPE   Col 1:11-14

May you be strengthened with all power, according to his glorious might, for all endurance and patience with joy, giving thanks to the Father, who has qualified us to share in the inheritance of the saints in light. He has delivered us from the dominion of darkness and transferred us to the kingdom of his beloved Son, in whom we have redemption, the forgiveness of sins.

'I have come to bear witness to the truth'

THE WORD IN THE GOSPEL   John 18:37

Pilate said to him, 'So you are a king?' Jesus answered,
'. . . For this I was born, and for this I have come into
the world, to bear witness to the truth.'

THE WORD IN THE PSALMS

Lord, hear a cause that is just,	16:1
pay heed to my cry.	
I have chosen the way of truth	118:30-32
with your decrees before me.	
I bind myself to do your will;	
Lord, do not disappoint me.	
I will run the way of your commands;	
you give freedom to my heart.	
O send forth your light and your truth;	42:3
let these be my guide.	
Let them bring me to your holy mountain	
to the place where you dwell.	
Lord, let your love come upon me,	118:41-43
the saving help of your promise.	
And I shall answer those who taunt me	
for I trust in your word.	
Do not take the word of truth from my mouth	
for I trust in your decrees.	

The Lord holds a cup in his hand,   74:9
    full of wine, foaming and spiced.
He pours it; they drink it to the dregs:
    all the wicked on the earth must drain it.

Whoever is wise, let him heed these things   106:43
    and consider the love of the Lord.

SILENT PRAYER

> Live in the truth and grow in holiness.
> I am with you always even to the end of time.

MEDITATION

Jesus chose the way of truth; indeed he was and is the Way and the Truth. That choice involved humbling himself in obedience to his Father's will and submitting to the abuse of judicial power by proud men. We too desire to choose the way of truth.

Therefore, grant us, Lord, realistic recognition of our own nothingness and our utter dependence on your generous love. May we perceive that truth entails suffering in sympathetic understanding with others.

Furthermore, by an ever deepening prayer life, let us search out the very nature of truth, the very person of Christ.

SILENT PRAYER

> Be consecrated in the truth.
> Your word, O Lord, is truth.

THE WORD OF HOPE   1 Tim 2:1-6a

First of all, then, I urge that supplications, prayers, intercessions, and thanksgivings be made for all men, for kings and all who are in high positions, that we may lead a quiet and peaceable life, godly and respectful in every way. This is good, and it is acceptable in the sight of God our Saviour, who desires all men to be saved and to come to the knowledge of the truth. For there is one God and there is one mediator between God and men, the man Christ Jesus who gave himself as a ransom for all.

'Everyone who is of the truth hears my voice'

THE WORD IN THE GOSPEL

John 18:37b

Jesus answered, 'Everyone who is of the truth hears my voice.'

THE WORD IN THE PSALMS

Lord, who shall be admitted to your tent? 14:1-3
    He who walks without fault;
    he who acts with justice
    and speaks the truth from his heart;
he who does not slander with his tongue.

Of this I am sure, that your love lasts for ever, 88:3,7,12
    that your truth is firmly established
    as the heavens.
Who in the skies can compare with the Lord?
    The heavens are yours, the world is yours.
    It is you who founded the earth
    and all it holds.
Your word, O Lord, for ever 118:89,90
    stands firm in the heavens:
your truth lasts from age to age,
    like the earth you created.

O God of truth, you detest 30:6-7
    those who worship false and empty gods.
Your justice I have proclaimed 39:10-12
    in the great assembly.
My lips I have not sealed;
    you know it, O Lord.
I have not hidden your justice in my heart
    but declared your faithful help.
I have not hidden your love and your truth
    from the great assembly.
O Lord, you will not withold
    your compassion from me.

Your merciful love and your truth
   always guard me.

SILENT PRAYER

Seek truth with all your heart.
Do not worship the false gods of modern society.

MEDITATION

Lord Jesus, between the agony in Gethsemane and the crucifixion on Calvary you highlighted for us the central position of truth. Again and again we read in the Gospels that you prayed. To follow your example will so train our spiritual ears that they may become finely tuned to your word. Then our lives, like yours, will flow from prayer.

May we become men and women of integrity who speak the truth in love and are responsive to your every desire. When circumstances demand, let us work zealously for the truth. It is our glory to persevere in God's service.

SILENT PRAYER

If you continue in my word, you are truly my disciples
and you will know the truth
and the truth will make you free.

THE WORD OF HOPE   1 Pet:1:13,22-23

Therefore gird up your minds, be sober, set your hope fully upon the grace that is coming to you at the revelation of Jesus Christ.

Having purified your souls by your obedience to the truth for a sincere love of the brethren, love one another earnestly from the heart. You have been born anew, not of perishable seed but of imperishable, through the living and abiding word of God.

'What is truth?'

THE WORD IN THE GOSPEL John 18:38a

Pilate said to him, 'What is truth?'

THE WORD IN THE PSALMS

Lead me, Lord, in your justice,   5:9-11
    because of those who lie in wait;
    make clear your way before me.
No truth can be found in their mouths,
    their heart is all mischief,
    their throat a wide-open grave,
    all honey their speech.
Declare them guilty, O God.
    Let them fail in their designs.

You are mighty, O Lord, and truth is
    your garment.   88:9
Turn your ear to my prayer: 16:1
    no deceit is on my lips.
O Lord, come to my rescue,   39:14
Lord, come to my aid.
From you may my judgement come forth.   16:2
Your eyes discern the truth.

The Lord sits enthroned for ever.   9:8-10
He has set up his throne for judgement;
he will judge the world with justice,
    he will judge the peoples with his truth.
For the oppressed let the Lord be a stronghold,
    a stronghold in times of distress.

The words of the Lord are words without alloy   11:7
    silver from the furnace, seven times refined.

SILENT PRAYER

God is truth.
A virtuous life leads us to the Truth.

MEDITATION

The calculating politician intent on preserving his power posed the question. The Word answered by voluntarily laying down his life from motives of pure love.

Grant, Lord, that we may steadily acquire an unerring, perhaps instinctive grasp of what constitutes reality in an unstable world. Unless we become as little children we may not enter the kingdom of truth, and the little child does know when it is loved by its father and mother. This is no weak starting point, for from it much may flow.

May we dwell constantly on your words so that they are refined within us some seventy times seven.

SILENT PRAYER

If we say we have no sin, we deceive ourselves
and the truth is not in us.
Jesus forgive us.

THE WORD OF HOPE   2 Cor 5:14-16a,17

For the love of Christ controls us, because we are convinced that one has died for all; therefore all have died. And he died for all that those who live might live no longer for themselves but for him who for their sake died and was raised.

From now on, therefore, we regard no one from a human point of view. Therefore, if any one is in Christ, he is a new creation; the old has passed away, behold, the new has come.

'I find no crime in him'

THE WORD IN THE GOSPEL   John 18:38b

Pilate went out to the Jews again, and told them,
'I find no crime in him.'

THE WORD IN THE PSALMS

The good man . . . conducts his affairs with
     honour   111:5,6,9
    The just man will never waver:
    his justice stands firm for ever.
His head will be raised in glory.

Can judges who do evil be your friends?   93:20,21
    They do injustice under cover of law;
    they attack the life of the just
    and condemn innocent blood.
It is you, O Lord, who are my hope,   70:5,6
    my trust, O Lord, since my youth.
On you I have leaned from my birth,
    from my mother's womb you have been my help.
My hope has always been in you.
Yes, it was you who took me from the womb,   21:10,11
    entrusted me to my mother's breast.
To you I was committed from my birth,
    from my mother's womb you have
    been my God.

As for me, the Lord will be a stronghold;   93:22
    my God will be the rock where I take refuge.
Long life to the Lord, my rock!   17:47,48
    Praised be the God who saves me,
    the God who gives me redress
    and subdues people under me.

SILENT PRAYER

Blessed are the pure of heart, they shall see God.
Seek the Way and the Life; protect the innocent.

MEDITATION

The hand of God has been guiding our lives from the first moment of our conception while, from the moment of our baptism we have been consecrated to the Lord. Our call is to holiness, to nurture the indwelling divine life so that no sin may be found in us.

Today 'innocent blood', the unborn child, is attacked and condemned; a mother may find it hard to resist social, economic or medical pressures. Let us never forget that Jesus, the pure lamb without spot or stain, died for all and shows us the power of his redeeming love. Lord, we pray for unborn children that at their birth they may be surrounded by love and security. May we receive the grace to live out our baptismal commitment to you.

SILENT PRAYER

I have come that you may have life
and have it more abundantly.
The innocent sing: Glory to you, O Lord.

THE WORD OF HOPE   Deut 7:6,9

For you are a people holy to the Lord your God; the Lord your God has chosen you to be a people for his own possession, out of all the peoples that are on the face of the earth. Know therefore that the Lord your God is God, the faithful God who keeps covenant and steadfast love with those who love him and keep his commandments to a thousand generations.

'Not this man, but Barabbas'

THE WORD IN THE GOSPEL   John 18:38-40

Pilate went out to the Jews again and told them, 'You
have a custom that I should release one man for you at
the Passover, will you have me release for you the King
of the Jews?' They cried out again, 'Not this man, but
Barabbas!' Now Barabbas was a robber.

THE WORD IN THE PSALMS

How long will you all attack one man   61:4
    to break him down,
as though he were a tottering wall,
    or a tumbling fence?

As for me, I trust in you, Lord,   30:15-16
    I say: 'You are my God.
My life is in your hands, deliver me
    from the hands of those who hate me.'
Hide me from the band of the wicked,   63:3
    from the throng of those who do evil.

O Lord, listen to my prayer   101:2,3
    and let my cry for help reach you.
Do not hide your face from me
    in the day of my distress.
Turn your ear towards me
    and answer me quickly when I call.
They may curse but you will bless.   108:28
O Lord, do not forsake me!   37:22
    My God, do not stay afar off!

In you I hope all day long   24:5-6
    because of your goodness, O Lord.
Remember your mercy, Lord,
    and the love you have shown from of old.

SILENT PRAYER

> This is my commandment, that you love one another
> as I have loved you.
> You are my friends if you do what I command you.

MEDITATION

The cause of Christ appears doomed. The crowd a mere few days earlier had taken palm branches and had gone out to meet Jesus, declaring, 'Hosanna; blessed is he who comes in the name of the Lord, even the King of Israel.' But now it has degenerated into a hostile and vicious mob. Modern crowds and public opinion remain equally fickle. Jesus was alone. He had been deserted by his closest friends, one had denied him and another had even betrayed him. Yet, though seemingly powerless his cause was with His Father, the Powerful One.

Lord, may we become other Christs. May we not become discouraged because the work of grace is a slow work. If our cause is with you, it cannot be withstood. Our trust rests in you.

SILENT PRAYER

> Open your ears to the voice from heaven
> that daily calls out:
> Do not harden your hearts.

THE WORD OF HOPE   Jas 1:2-4

Count it all joy, my brethren, when you meet various trials, for you know that the testing of your faith produces steadfastness. And let steadfastness have its full effect, that you may be perfect and complete, lacking in nothing.

Jesus was scourged

THE WORD IN THE GOSPEL   John 19:1

Then Pilate took Jesus and scourged him.

THE WORD IN THE PSALMS

All my frame burns with fever;   37:8,11
    all my body is sick.
My heart throbs, my strength is spent;
    the very light has gone from my eyes.
My days are vanishing like smoke,   101:4
    my bones burn away like a fire.

I call to you, Lord, all the day long.   87:10-13,15-16
Will you work your wonders for the dead?
    Will the shades stand and praise you?
Will your love be told in the grave
    or your faithfulness among the dead?
Will your wonders be known in the dark
    or your justice in the land of oblivion?
Lord, why do you reject me?
    Why do you hide your face?
Wretched, close to death from my youth,
    I have born your trials; I am numb.

He will conceal you with his pinions   90:4,11
    and under his wings you will find refuge.
For you has he commanded his angels,
    to keep you in all your ways.

SILENT PRAYER

    Behold the suffering servant.
    I confess that I have sinned through my own fault.

MEDITATION

As we suffer a scourging in body or mind and as, through the mass media, we perceive Jesus being scourged today in so many who are subjected to various forms of physical and mental torture, our natural instinct is to question, even to question the goodness of God. With our finite minds we do not select pain as our first choice. Yet, when we look with the eyes of faith we come to understand how Jesus has enfolded pain in a cocoon of love and has revealed the treasure within.

Grant, Lord, that we may not reject this source of grace. Let us support the suffering by our prayer.

SILENT PRAYER

If you love Jesus with all your heart and understanding, you are not far from the kingdom.

THE WORD OF HOPE   1 Pet 4:13-14

Rejoice in so far as you share in Christ's sufferings, that you may also rejoice and be glad when his glory is revealed. If you are reproached for the name of Christ, you are blessed, because the spirit of glory and of God rests upon you.

A crown of thorns was put on his head

THE WORD IN THE GOSPEL   John 19:2

And the soldiers plaited a crown of thorns, and put it on his head, and arrayed him in a purple robe.

THE WORD IN THE PSALMS

The Lord swore an oath to David;   131:11,17,18
    he will not go back on his word:
'A son, the fruit of your body,
    will I set upon your throne.
David's stock will flower:
    I will prepare a lamp for my anointed.
I will cover his enemies with shame,
    but on him my crown shall shine.'

O Lord, remember David;   131:1,10
    do not reject your anointed.
It is for you that I suffer taunts,   68:8,10
    that shame covers my face.
I burn with zeal for your house
    and taunts against you fall on me.
I pray: 'Do not let them mock me,   37:17,18
    those who triumph if my foot should slip.'
For I am on the point of falling
    and my pain is always before me.
Out of the depths I cry to you, O Lord,   129:1,2
    Lord, hear my voice!
O let your ears be attentive
    to the voice of my pleading.
This is my prayer to you,   68:14
    my prayer for your favour.
In your great love, answer me, O God,
    with your help that never fails.

May the Lord be blessed day after day.   67:20
    He bears our burdens, God our saviour.

SILENT PRAYER

    Behold the King of sorrow and of love
    He is suffering for my sake.

MEDITATION

Jesus our Saviour, his kingship scorned, bears our burdens. His prayer to his Father that this chalice of suffering might be removed seems unanswered as the events of his sacred Passion unfold with one horror following another. However, there is no such thing as unanswered prayer. Only the nature and the timing of the answer may surprise and are not fully visible from this side of the grave. The glory of Christ's universal kingship is thus hidden.

    Lord Jesus, may we never cease to acknowledge you as King of the universe with dominion over all creation. You are the Alpha and the Omega. We trust your answer to our prayer since it cannot but be an expression of your love.

SILENT PRAYER

    He is the Wonderful Counsellor and the Prince of Peace.
    Indeed he bears our burdens.

THE WORD OF HOPE   Rom 8:18-21

I consider that the sufferings of this present time are not worth comparing with the glory that is to be revealed to us. For the creation waits with eager longing for the revealing of the sons of God; for the creation was subjected to futility, not of its own will but by the will of him who subjected it in hope; because the creation itself will be set free from its bondage to decay and obtain the glorious liberty of the children of God.

'Hail, King of the Jews!'

(The soldiers) came up to him, saying, 'Hail, King of
the Jews!' and struck him with their hands.

THE WORD IN THE PSALMS

Can he who made the ear, not hear?   93:9
Can he who made the eye, not see?
See how they gabble open-mouthed;   58: 8
   their lips are filled with insults.
   'For who,' they say, 'will hear us?'
Then they make me a byword,   68:12,13
   the gossip of men at the gates,
   the subject of drunkards' songs.

A mighty God is the Lord,   94:3
   a great king above all gods.
High above all nations is the Lord,   112:4
   above the heavens his glory.
God is king over the nations;   46:9,10
   God reigns on his holy throne.
The rulers of the earth belong to God;
   to God who reigns over all.

Evening, morning and at noon   54:18,19
   I will cry and lament.
He will deliver my soul in peace
   in the attack against me:
for those who fight me are many,
   but he hears my voice.
It is the Lord who grants favours to those   4:4
   whom he loves,
   the Lord hears me whenever I call him.

SILENT PRAYER

> He is the Almighty King.
> Offer him true homage.

MEDITATION

Each independent nation state pursuing its own policies cannot resolve many modern issues. Among these are the threat of global environmental pollution, international terrorism or nuclear holocaust. As the psalmist declares: 'God is king over the nations'.

Let us pray for Christians throughout the world and their witness to the international kingship of Christ. As we intercede, 'deliver us from evil', may we remember that Christ, the whole Christ, is the sole answer.

Lord, grant us the grace to fully utilise any opportunities for creating an atmosphere conducive to peace in our families and our communities. May international peace-keeping forces and relief organising agencies be blessed in their endeavours.

We recognise that yours is a kingdom of holiness, life and love.

SILENT PRAYER

> Help us to live by the Gospel of Christ,
> the King of all creation.
> Lord, we acclaim your glory.

THE WORD OF HOPE   Dan 6:26b-27a

His kingdom shall never be destroyed,
    and his dominion shall be to the end.
He delivers and rescues,
    he works signs and wonders
    in heaven and on earth.

'Here is the man!'

THE WORD IN THE GOSPEL

John 19:5

So Jesus came out, wearing the crown of thorns and the purple robe. Pilate said to them, 'Here is the man!'

THE WORD IN THE PSALMS

You do not ask for holocaust and victim.   39:7-9
    Instead, here am I.
In the scroll of the book it stands written
    that I should do your will.
My God, I delight in your law
    in the depth of my heart.

Lord, you are just indeed;   118:137,138,111,114
    your decrees are right.   116-118
You have imposed your will with justice
    and with absolute truth.
Your will is my heritage for ever,
    the joy of my heart.
You are my shelter, my shield;
    I hope in your word.
If you uphold me by your promise I shall live;
    let my hopes not be in vain.
Sustain me and I shall be saved;
    their cunning is in vain.

In God alone is my soul at rest;   61:2,3
    my help comes from him.
He alone is my rock, my stronghold,
    my fortress: I stand firm.

SILENT PRAYER

    Prayer is an offering of self to God.
    We bring to you your gifts to us.

MEDITATION

Ecce homo! Behold the man! Let us recognise the plight of suffering humanity – the battered baby and the abused child, the victim of famine and the frail geriatric. Let us also acknowledge that trials are inevitable for the Christian searching for God's will, both its essence and the best means of pursuing it. If we feel ourselves vulnerable, we know that Christ was. The demands of sharing in his sufferings have to be faced, but the way of the Cross is a sure though long road.

Let us pray for all enduring terrible suffering and all deprived of their human rights and dignity.

Lord, we offer ourselves saying, 'Here am I'.

SILENT PRAYER

Speak, Lord, your servant is listening.
You have the message of eternal life.

THE WORD OF HOPE   Heb 4:14-16

Since then we have a great high priest who has passed through the heavens, Jesus, the Son of God, let us hold fast our confession. For we have not a high priest who is unable to sympathise with our weaknesses, but one who in every respect has been tempted as we are, yet without sinning. Let us then with confidence draw near to the throne of grace, that we may receive mercy and find grace to help in time of need.

'Crucify him, crucify him!'

THE WORD IN THE GOSPEL   John 19:6a

When the chief priests and officers saw him, they cried
out, 'Crucify him, crucify him!'

THE WORD IN THE PSALMS

I tremble at the shouts of the foe,   54:3,4,17
   at the cries of the wicked;
   for they bring down evil upon me.
They assail me with fury.
As for me, I will cry to God
   and the Lord will save me.

O God, do not keep silent,   82:2,3
   do not be dumb and unmoved, O God,
   for your enemies raise a tumult.
Those who hate you lift up their heads.
Arise, O God, and defend your cause!   73:22,23
   Remember how the senseless revile you all the day.
   Do not forget the clamour of your foes.
Do not let the deep engulf me   68:16
   nor death close its mouth on me.

Awake, stir to my defence,   34:23-25,27
   to my cause, O God!
Vindicate me, Lord, in your justice,
   do not let them rejoice.
Do not let them think: 'Yes! We have won,
   we have brought him to an end!'
Let there be joy for those who love my cause.

SILENT PRAYER

   The Lord speaks to the quiet heart.
   Forgive our impatient words and restless or
     angry moods.

MEDITATION

A crowd may become a mob. Law and order on which the citizen is so dependent may be restored. A Christian's heart may be filled with raucous clamour. A greater peace-keeping exercise may be carried out as the mind resists temptation, so that spiritual calm returns to the heart. Caught off guard our sin may crucify the Lord whom we profess to love.

Let us possess our souls in patience and contain our hearts and minds within the discipline of wisdom. Lord, do not let me be engulfed by the tumult either from without or from within. Lord, graciously hear me.

SILENT PRAYER

Waste no time on idle day dreams or noisy diversions. Concentrate on what is truly good.

THE WORD OF HOPE   John 12:24-25

Truly, truly, I say to you, unless a grain of wheat falls into the earth and dies, it remains alone; but if it dies, it bears much fruit. He who loves his life loses it, and he who hates his life in this world will keep it for eternal life.

'Power over me has been given you from above'

THE WORD IN THE GOSPEL   John 19:9-11a

Pilate entered the praetorium again and said to Jesus, 'Where are you from?' But Jesus gave no answer. Pilate therefore said to him, 'You will not speak to me? Do you not know that I have power to release you, and power to crucify you?' Jesus answered him, 'You would have no power over me unless it had been given you from above.'

THE WORD IN THE PSALMS

Your throne, O God, shall endure for ever.	44:7,8
A sceptre of justice is the sceptre of your kingdom.	
Your love is for justice; your hatred for evil.	
Lord, . . . let the nations know they are but men.	9:21
Justice and right are the pillars of your throne,	88:15
love and truth walk in your presence.	
The Lord is king for ever and ever.	9,10:16
The heathen shall perish from the land he rules.	
Praise God in his holy place,	150:1
praise him in his mighty heavens.	
He rules for ever by his might.	65:7
His eyes keep watch over the nations:	
let rebels not rise against him.	
He frustrates the designs of the nations,	32:10,11
he defeats the plans of the peoples.	
His own designs shall stand for ever,	
the plans of his heart from age to age.	
He shall break the power of the wicked,	74:11
while the strength of the just shall be exalted.	
I love you, Lord, my strength,	17:2-4
my rock, my fortress, my saviour.	

My God is the rock where I take refuge;
   my shield, my mighty help, my stronghold.
The Lord is worthy of all praise:
   when I call I am saved from my foes.

Silent Prayer

I surrender myself into your hands, O Lord.
You are my secure stronghold.

Meditation

Christ humbled himself as his Father willed and was obedient even unto death. God is above all, guiding all by his spirit, a spirit of love. We have at least influence and perhaps power over others, so let us remember that they were given to us from above; if we wish to use them, let us recall the Beatitudes, the Great Charter of the Kingdom. There we learn that among the blessed are those who hunger and thirst for righteousness, the poor in spirit, the meek and the merciful. May we seek to work responsibly and in harmony with the designs of Jesus. Grant, Lord, the inner strength to pursue the way of humility.

Silent Prayer

Blessed are the poor in spirit, for theirs
is the kingdom of heaven.
Blessed are the meek, for they shall inherit the earth.

The Word Of Hope
1 Pet 5:5b-7

Clothe yourselves, all of you, with humility toward one another, for 'God opposes the proud, but gives grace to the humble.'

Humble yourselves therefore under the mighty hand of God, that in due time he may exalt you. Cast all your anxieties on him, for he cares about you.

Pilate handed him over to be crucified

THE WORD IN THE GOSPEL   John 19:15b-16

Pilate said to them, 'Shall I crucify your King?' The chief priests answered, 'We have no king but Caesar.' Then he handed him over to be crucified.

THE WORD IN THE PSALMS

'With my chosen one I have made a covenant;   88:4,5
     I have sworn to David my servant:
I will establish your dynasty for ever
     and set up your throne through all ages.'

And yet you have spurned, rejected,   88:39,40,43,45
     you are angry with the one you
     have anointed.
You have broken your covenant with
     your servant
     and dishonoured his crown in the dust.
You have exalted the right hand of his foes;
     you have made all his enemies rejoice.
You have brought his glory to an end;
     you have hurled his throne to the ground.
Who understands the power of your anger   89:11,13
     and fears the strength of your fury?
Lord, relent! Is your anger for ever?   89:13
O Lord God of hosts, hear my prayer,   83:9
     give ear, O God of Jacob.
O God, give your judgement to the king.   71:1

Those who seek to destroy my life   62:10-11
     shall go down to the depths of the earth.
They shall be put into the power of the sword
     and left as the prey of the jackals.

As for me, the Lord will be a stronghold;   93:22
My God will be the rock where I
    take refuge.

SILENT PRAYER

Renounce the world and its distorted values.
Gaze on the One who will reign for ever,

MEDITATION

The chief priests answered in a way they knew to be
politically expedient and the scene was being set for the
King of David's line to take up the cross, the sceptre of
his power. We who are sinners deserved the cross, but it
was our Saviour who accepted it. To follow in his
footsteps and take up our own personal crosses each
day presents a permanent challenge.

May we live in accordance with enlightening
Christian principles rather than dubious secular
expediency. Let us renounce worldly manoeuvres.
Grant us, Lord, an ever-deepening understanding of the
saving power of the cross.

SILENT PRAYER

By your cross you have wondrously redeemed us.
The way of humility is your way.

THE WORD OF HOPE   1 Cor 1:18-19

For the word of the cross is folly to those who are
perishing, but to us who are being saved it is the power
of God. For it is written,
   'I will destroy the wisdom of the wise,
   and the cleverness of the clever I will thwart.'

He bore his own cross
to Golgotha

THE WORD IN THE GOSPEL John 19:17

So they took Jesus, and he went out, bearing his own cross to the place called the place of the skull, which is called in Hebrew Golgotha.

THE WORD IN THE PSALMS

I am bowed and brought to my knees. 37:7
  I go mourning all the day long.
Many bulls have surrounded me, 21:13,14,22,23
  fierce bulls of Bashan close me in.
Against me they open wide their jaws,
  like lions rending and roaring.
Save my life from the jaws of these lions,
  my poor soul from the horns of these oxen.
I will tell of your name to my brethren
  and praise you where they are assembled.

Spent and utterly crushed 37:9
  I cry aloud in anguish of heart.
Have mercy on me, Lord, I have no strength; 6:3,4
  Lord, heal me, my body is racked;
my soul is racked with pain.

The Lord guides the steps of a man 36:23,24
  and makes safe the path of one he loves.
Though he stumble he shall never fall
  for the Lord holds him by the hand.

When I think: 'I have lost my foothold'; 93:18-19
  your mercy, Lord, holds me up.
When cares increase in my heart
  your consolation calms my soul.

SILENT PRAYER

> Help us to bear one another's burdens.
> Save us, Lord, by the power of your wondrous cross.

MEDITATION

In compassion Jesus carried our sorrows and he loved us whom he was carrying along the way. If we are to be worthy of him we must follow the glorious conqueror who nobly bore the standard of his victory. The road to the summit of perfection is uphill. At the start its gradient looks dauntingly steep, but as we advance our pace will quicken .

Grant, Lord, that your divine love may be the very air we breathe on life's journey. Jesus ever rich in mercy, receive our thanks and our prayers.

SILENT PRAYER

> Hail holy cross, standard of victory.
> Let the enemies of the Lord flee before him.

THE WORD OF HOPE   Mt 11:28-30

Come to me, all who labour and are heavy laden, and I will give you rest. Take my yoke upon you, and learn from me; for I am gentle and lowly in heart, and you will find rest for your souls. For my yoke is easy, and my burden is light.

'Daughters of Jerusalem, ... weep for yourselves and for your children'

THE WORD IN THE GOSPEL   Luke 23:27-28

And there followed him a great multitude of the people, and of women who bewailed and lamented him. But Jesus turning to them said, 'Daughters of Jerusalem, do not weep for me, but weep for yourselves and for your children.'

THE WORD IN THE PSALMS

O Lord, remember me   105:4
    out of the love you have for your people.

By the rivers of Babylon   136:1-4
    there we sat and wept,
    remembering Zion;
on the poplars that grew there
    we hung up our harps.
For it was there that they asked us,
    our captors, for songs,
    our oppressors, for joy.
O how could we sing
    the song of the Lord
    on alien soil?
For you, O God, have tested us,   65:10-12
    you have tried us as silver is tried.
    you led us, God, into the snare,
    you laid a heavy burden on our backs.
You let men ride over our heads;
    we went through fire and through water
    but then you brought us relief.

O Lord, you have been our refuge   89:1-2
    from one generation to the next.
Before the mountains were born
    or the earth or the world brought forth,

you are God, without beginning or end.
In your goodness, show favour to Zion.   50:20

From Zion may the Lord be blessed,   134:21
    he who dwells in Jerusalem.

SILENT PRAYER

    Lord, do not forget your people.
    Comfort the sorrowful, bring peace to all.

MEDITATION

The Word was born of a woman, Mary, full of grace and
comforter of the afflicted. The daughters of Jerusalem
wept as previous generations had done and as future
ones would do. On the summit of Calvary a group of
holy women were to keep vigil in silent grief.

    Let us pray for all who are weeping today – the
oppressed, the bereaved and those watching their loved
ones suffer. May the qualities of compassion and
sensitivity be developed in our own hearts so that our
touch may be healing and may renew the face of the
earth.

SILENT PRAYER

    You gave Mary to us as our loving mother.
    Through her prayers console the distressed.

THE WORD OF HOPE   Is 65:19,23-24;

I will rejoice in Jerusalem,
    and be glad in my people,
no more shall be heard in it the sound of weeping
    and the cry of distress.
They shall not labour in vain,
    or bear children for calamity;
for they shall be the offspring of the blessed of the Lord,
    and their children with them.
Before they call I will answer,
    while they are yet speaking I will hear.

They crucified him

THE WORD IN THE GOSPEL   John 19:18,23-24a

There they crucified him, and with him two others, one on either side and Jesus between them.

When the soldiers had crucified Jesus they took his garments and made four parts, one for each soldier; also his tunic. But the tunic was without seam, woven from top to bottom; so they said to one another, 'Let us not tear it, but cast lots for it to see whose it shall be.'

THE WORD IN THE PSALMS

Like water I am poured out,   21:15-17,21
   disjointed are all my bones.
My heart has become like wax,
   it is melted within my breast.
Parched as burnt clay is my throat,
   my tongue cleaves to my jaws.
Many dogs have surrounded me,
   a band of the wicked beset me.
They tear holes in my hands and my feet
   and lay me in the dust of death.
Rescue my soul from the sword,
   my life from the grip of these dogs.

Have mercy on me, O Lord,   30:10-11
   for I am in distress.
Tears have wasted my eyes,
   my throat and my heart.

For my life is spent with sorrow
   and my years with sighs.
Affliction has broken down my strength
   and my bones waste away.

I can count every one of my bones.   21:18
   These people stare at me and gloat.
My wounds are foul and festering.   37:6

They divide my clothing among them.   21:19
    They cast lots for my robe.
Long have I known that your will   118:152
    is established for ever.

SILENT PRAYER

> Greater love than this has no one.
> Be nailed to the cross with Christ.

MEDITATION

The Word was made flesh, dwelt among us and was crucified by us. Jesus, the Immortal Lord, who is Life itself, assumed our mortality so that he might die for us and by his death might slay our death. Let us repeatedly set ourselves to know Christ Crucified.

Grant, Lord, that we may steadily die to self will. May we discipline our minds and our bodies, rejecting the blind pursuit of pleasures and worldly position. May we become people who experience the glorious liberty of the children of God. Let us pray for all suffering emotional, psychological and physical wounds. Lord, grant healing to all.

SILENT PRAYER

> A spirit of love and forgiveness has been poured out.
> Stand with Mary and John at the foot of the cross.

THE WORD OF HOPE   1 John 1:1-3

That which was from the beginning, which we have heard, which we have seen with our eyes, which we have looked upon and touched with our hands, concerning the word of life – the life was made manifest and we saw it, and testify to it, and proclaim to you the eternal life which was with the Father and was made manifest to us – that which we have seen and heard we proclaim also to you, so that you may have fellowship with us; and our fellowship is with the Father and with his Son Jesus Christ.

'Jesus of Nazareth,
the king of the Jews'

John 19:19

Pilate also wrote a title and put it on the cross; it read,
'Jesus of Nazareth, the King of the Jews.'

THE WORD IN THE PSALMS

The Lord will wield from Zion   109:2,3
    your sceptre of power:
    rule in the midst of all your foes.
A prince from the day of your birth
    on the holy mountains;
    from the womb before the dawn I begot you.

The Lord is king . . .   96:1,3,4
A fire prepares his path;
    it burns up his foes on every side.
His lightnings light up the world,
    the earth trembles at the sight.
He pours contempt upon princes,   106:40,39,41,42
    makes them wander in trackless wastes.
They diminish, are reduced to nothing
    by oppression, evil and sorrow.
But he raises the needy from distress.
The upright see it and rejoice,
    but all who do wrong are silenced.

Those who put their trust in the Lord   124:1,2
    are like Mount Zion, that cannot be shaken,
    that stands for ever.
Jerusalem! The mountains surround her,
    so the Lord surrounds his people
    both now and forever.
As for me in my poverty and pain   68:30
    let your help, O God, lift me up.

SILENT PRAYER

> The sovereignty of the Crucified is revealed.
> Hour by hour place your trust in him.

MEDITATION

The cynical Pilate who had queried the very possibility of truth now wrote it at the end of what had been for him a deeply troublesome judicial case. We acknowledge the sovereignty of the Crucified, the king of all nations.

You, Lord, are the prince of peace born in Bethlehem. Your kingdom is established in justice and integrity. May we become your loyal subjects raising from distress the needy, be they hungry, thirsty or naked, be they strangers, prisoners or the sick. You, Lord, are the one who is to come in glory. We long to hear you say to us, 'As you did it to one of the least of these my brethren, you did it to me.'

SILENT PRAYER

> Then the King will say to those at his right hand,
> 'Come, O blessed of my Father, inherit the kingdom
> prepared for you from the foundation of the world.'

THE WORD OF HOPE   Eph 5:1-2

Therefore be imitators of God, as beloved children. And walk in love, as Christ loved us and gave himself up for us, a fragrant offering and sacrifice to God.

93

They derided him

THE WORD IN THE GOSPEL   Mark 15:29-30

And those who passed by derided him, wagging their
heads, and saying, 'Aha! You would destroy the temple
and build it in three days, save yourself, and come
down from the cross!'

THE WORD IN THE PSALMS

Now that I am in trouble they gather,   34:15-16
    they gather and mock me.
They take me by surprise and strike me
    and tear me to pieces.
They provoke me with mockery on mockery
    and gnash their teeth.
I am a worm and no man,   21:7
    the butt of men, laughing stock of the people.
All day long my foes revile me;   101:9
    those who hate me use my name as a curse.
In the face of all my foes   30:12
    I am a reproach,
an object of scorn to my neighbours
    and of fear to my friends.
See how many are my foes;   24:19
    how violent their hatred for me.

How long, O Lord? Will you be angry for ever,   78:5
    how long will your anger burn like fire?
Do not leave me alone in my distress;   21:12
    come close, there is none else to help.

My soul shall be joyful in the Lord   34:9-10
    and rejoice in his salvation.
My whole being will say:
    'Lord, who is like you
    who rescue the weak from the strong
    and the poor from the oppressor?'

Silent Prayer

See the sublime humility of Christ,
the scorn of the people.
He came not to condemn but to save sinners.

Meditation

Totally one of us, Christ suffered pain and derision. He who is Love challenges us to endure as He did and to love him in return. Everyone, no matter how weak, is offered a share in the victory of the cross. Let us renew again and again the offering of our very selves to God.

May my soul be a pure offering and a pleasing sacrifice; may this prayer resonate in the depths of my being.

Grant us, Lord, the grace of fidelity when we are derided. Forgive us for the occasions on which we have regarded others with scorn or contempt.

Let us pray for teenagers and young people ridiculed by their peer group for the expression of Christian values.

Silent Prayer

The Lord is abounding in love and tender compassion.
Christ endured the cross for the sake of the joy
that lay before him.

The Word Of Hope   Acts 4:11-12

This is the stone rejected by you builders, but which has become the head of the corner. And there is salvation in no one else, for there is no other name under heaven given among men by which we must be saved.

'He saved others;
he cannot save himself'

So also the chief priests mocked him to one another with the scribes, saying, 'He saved others; he cannot save himself. Let the Christ, the King of Israel, come down now from the cross, that we may see and believe.'

THE WORD IN THE PSALMS

All who see me deride me.   21:8,9
    They curl their lips, they toss their heads.
'He trusted in the Lord, let him save him;
    let him release him if this is his friend.'

How long, O God, is the enemy to scoff?   73:10
    Is the foe to insult your name for ever?
How long, O Lord? Will you hide yourself   88:47-51
    for ever?
    How long will your anger burn like a fire?
Remember, Lord, . . .
    how frail you have made the sons of men.
What man can live and never see death?
    Who can save himself from the grasp of the grave?
Where are your mercies of the past, O Lord,
    which you have sworn in your faithfulness to David?
Remember, Lord, how your servant is taunted,
    how I have to bear all the insults of the peoples.

How many are my foes, O Lord!   3:2-5
How many are rising up against me!
How many are saying about me:
    'There is no help for him in God.'
But you, Lord, are a shield about me,
    my glory, who lift up my head.

I cry aloud to the Lord.
  He answers from his holy mountain.

SILENT PRAYER

We believe that Jesus was made man and was crucified
for our salvation.
Jesus, we trust in your mercy.

MEDITATION

How long is suffering to persist in our world? How
many are rising up against us! We understand the
psalmist's question and sentiments. The world is filled
with sin and sin always produces suffering. May
Christians resist the assaults of the world, both its
obvious direct hits and, more dangerously, its subtle
subversive scorn. Let us place our total confidence in
Christ because it is He who has overcome the world.

Lord, may we lean away from whatever is not
conducive to love of you. Grant us great prudence in
our relationships with people and with things.

Deliberately, thoughtfully and wholeheartedly may
we seek Christ our Saviour.

SILENT PRAYER

Gaze on Jesus Crucified:
recognise in him our own humanity and find God.
He is healing our wounds.

THE WORD OF HOPE   Heb 10:35-37

Therefore do not throw away your confidence, which
has a great reward. For you have need of endurance, so
that you may do the will of God and receive what is
promised.

'For yet a little while,
  and the coming one shall come and shall not tarry.'

'Today you will be
with me in paradise'

THE WORD IN THE GOSPEL   Luke 23:42-43

And (one of the criminals put to death with him) said,
'Jesus, remember me when you come in kingly power.'
And he said to him, 'Truly, I say to you, today you will
be with me in Paradise.'

THE WORD IN THE PSALMS

To you all flesh will come   64:3,4
    with its burden of sin.

The Lord has set his sway in heaven   102:19,8-14,17
    and his kingdom is ruling over all.
The Lord is compassion and love,
    slow to anger and rich in mercy.
His wrath will come to an end;
    he will not be angry for ever.
He does not treat us according to our sins
    nor repay us according to our faults.
For as the heavens are high above the earth
    so strong is his love for those who fear him.
As far as the east is from the west
    so far does he remove our sins.
As a father has compassion on his sons,
    the Lord has pity on those who fear him;
for he knows of what we are made,
    he remembers that we are dust.
The love of the Lord is everlasting
    on those who hold him in fear.

God gives the lonely a home to live in;   67:7
    he leads the prisoners forth into freedom.
O Lord, your strength gives joy to the king.   20:2

SILENT PRAYER

Lord, remember me when you come into
your kingdom.
Remove the crushing burden of our guilt.

MEDITATION

The thief confessed his sins and laid aside their burden.
O Jesus, remember me when you come into your
kingdom; the request opened paradise. The Word spoke
and he is the beloved Son in whom the Father is well
pleased. The Lord does not desire a sinner's death, but
his conversion. Let us turn to him, implore his mercy
and live.

Lord, may our annual Lenten observance be a
channel of your grace and may the remembrance of
your passion and death each Friday throughout the year
bring us closer to the coming of the kingdom. Let us
steadfastly resolve to express sorrow for our own sins
by prayer, fasting and almsgiving.

SILENT PRAYER

O Lord, I am truly sorry for my sins;
they have crucified you and offended
your infinite goodness.

THE WORD OF HOPE   Is, 61:1-2a

The Spirit of the Lord God is upon me,
because the Lord has anointed me
to bring good tidings to the afflicted,
he has sent me to bind up the brokenhearted,
to proclaim liberty to the captives,
and the opening of the prison to those who are bound;
to proclaim the year of the Lord's favour.

Darkness covered the land

THE WORD IN THE GOSPEL   Mark 15:33

And when the sixth hour had come, there was darkness
over the whole land until the ninth hour.

THE WORD IN THE PSALMS

He sent darkness, and dark was made.   104:28

Behind and before you besiege me,   138:5,11,12
    your hand ever laid upon me.
If I say: 'Let the darkness hide me,'
    even darkness is not dark for you.
Yours is the day and yours is the night   73:16

See the wicked bracing their bow;   10:2,4,5,7
    they are fixing their arrow on the string
    to shoot upright men in the dark.
The Lord is in his holy temple,
    the Lord, whose throne is in heaven.
His eyes look down on the world;
    his gaze tests mortal men.
The Lord tests the just and the wicked:
    the lover of violence he hates.
The Lord is just and loves justice:
    the upright shall see his face.

My God, the sons of men   35:8
    find refuge in the shelter of your wings.
Your word is a lamp for my steps   118:105
    and a light for my path.
In you is the source of life   35:10
and in your light we see light.

SILENT PRAYER

The darkness will yield to the true light of day.
Jesus be a light for my path.

MEDITATION

Light can always penetrate the stifling darkness of this
world's estrangement from God. Snatched, as we are,
from the powers of darkness may we recognise our role
in society. We reject ill-considered exploitation which
risks destroying the planet and we long to bequeath to
generations yet unborn a spiritual environment which
manifests the glory of God.

Light-bearing Christ, enlighten us and all men and
women of good will. Grant that a spark of your light
may penetrate the hearts of those of ill will. May we
perceive, as Mary did, during her vigil beside the cross,
that out of darkness light is born.

SILENT PRAYER

Mother of Mercy, full of divine light,
intercede for us with your Son.
Consider our interior difficulties and sufferings.

THE WORD OF HOPE   1 John 1:5,7

This is the message we have heard from him and
proclaim to you, that God is light and in him is no
darkness at all. If we walk in the light, as he is in the
light, we have fellowship with one another, and the
blood of Jesus his Son cleanses us from all sin.

'My God, my God, why have you forsaken me?'

THE WORD IN THE GOSPEL   Mark 15:34

And at the ninth hour Jesus cried with a loud voice,
'Eloi, Eloi, lama sabachthani?' which means 'My God,
my God, why have you forsaken me?'

THE WORD IN THE PSALMS

With cries that pierce me to the heart,
    my enemies revile me,
saying to me all the day long;
    'Where is your God?'
	41:11

Look on my right and see: 141:5
    there is no one who takes my part.
I have no means of escape,
    not one who cares for my soul.
My friends avoid me like a leper;   37:12
    those closest to me stand afar off.

Taunts have broken my heart;   68:21-22
    I have reached the end of my strength.
I looked in vain for compassion,
    for consolers; not one could I find.
In my thirst they gave me vinegar to drink.
I fade like an evening shadow;   108:23
    my life is on the brink of the grave.   87:4

With all my voice I cry to the Lord,   141:2
    with all my voice I entreat the Lord.
O my God, I call by day and you give no reply,   21:3
Your arrows have sunk deep in me;   37:3
    your hand has come down upon me.
My God, my God, why have you forsaken me?   21:2
    You are far from my plea and the cry of my distress.

SILENT PRAYER

Behold him without beauty.
He who is infinite loveliness was thus brought low.

MEDITATION

Fixing the eyes of our heart on Jesus crucified we recognise in him our own humanity and watch life and death contending. As suffering and a sense of abandonment increased, obedience was being perfected; he was bringing us healing and taking away our sins. Life's own Author was on the point of being slain and yet, 'combat strangely ended', today he lives to draw all things to himself.

Help us, Lord, to prepare ourselves for any terrible suffering, be it physical, mental, moral or spiritual, which it is your will to bestow on us. Mary, Mother of Wisdom, was thus prepared and therefore was to be found in her place at the foot of the cross.

Let us discard any illusions about our own goodness since self-centredness is poisoning and we are utterly dependent on you, O Lord.

SILENT PRAYER

Persevere in obedience to his will.
Repent, avoid all deliberate sin and seek salvation.

THE WORD OF HOPE   Rom 5:8-9

God shows his love for us in that while we were yet sinners Christ died for us. Since, therefore, we are now justified by his blood, much more shall we be saved by him from the wrath of God.

'Father, into your hands
I commend my spirit'

THE WORD IN THE GOSPEL   Luke 23: 46

Then Jesus, crying with a loud voice, said, 'Father, into your hands I commend my spirit!' And having said this he breathed his last.

THE WORD IN THE PSALMS

My soul is longing for the Lord   129:6
    more than watchman for daybreak.

Let my prayer come into your presence.   87:3
    O turn your ear to my cry.
Let your sword rescue my soul from the wicked, 16:13,14
    let your hand, O Lord, rescue me from men.
Help me, Lord my God   108:26
    save me because of your love.

In you, O Lord, I take refuge.   30:2-6
    Let me never be put to shame.
In your justice, set me free,
    hear me and speedily rescue me.
Be a rock of refuge for me,
    a mighty stronghold to save me,
    for you are my rock, my stronghold.
For your name's sake, lead me and guide me.
Release me from the snares they have hidden
    for you are my refuge Lord.

Into your hands I commend my spirit.
It is you who will redeem me, Lord.

SILENT PRAYER

Into your hands I commend myself,
body,
soul and spirit.
Redeem me, O Lord.

MEDITATION

The innocent victim dying on the cross at Calvary is also the great High Priest, offering himself to the Father.

With so merciful and faithful a high priest let us offer ourselves, body, soul and spirit, for the redemption of many.

In all the circumstances of our daily lives may we live out this total self-giving.

Father, grant that our hidden selves may grow strong. May we die to sin and live for holiness.

SILENT PRAYER

It is accomplished.
This is the time to win God's blessing.

THE WORD OF HOPE   Eph 3:14b-19

I bow my knees before the Father, from whom every family in heaven and on earth is named, that according to the riches of his glory he may grant you to be strengthened with might through his Spirit in the inner man, and that Christ may dwell in your hearts through faith; that you, being rooted and grounded in love, may have power to comprehend with all the saints what is the breadth and length and height and depth, and to know the love of Christ which surpasses knowledge, that you may be filled with all the fullness of God.

The earth shook

THE WORD IN THE GOSPEL   Matt 27:51

And behold, the curtain of the temple was torn in two, from top to bottom; and the earth shook, and the rocks were split.

THE WORD IN THE PSALMS

You have made the earth quake, torn it open.   59:4
Tremble, O earth, before the Lord,   113:7
   in the presence of the God of Jacob.

'When I reach the appointed time,   74:3-8
   then I will judge with justice.
Though the earth and all who dwell in it may rock,
   it is I who uphold its pillars.
To the boastful I say: 'Do not boast,'
   to the wicked: 'Do not flaunt your strength,
   do not flaunt your strength on high.
   Do not speak with insolent pride.'
For neither from the east nor from the west,
   nor from the desert or mountains
   comes judgement,
but God himself is the judge.
   One he humbles, another he exalts.
The Lord will bless those who fear him,   113:13
   the little no less than the great.

I cry to you, O Lord,   141:6
I have said : 'You are my refuge,
   all I have in the land of the living.'

Nations are in tumult, kingdoms are shaken;   45:7,11
   he lifts his voice, the earth shrinks away.
'Be still and know that I am God,
   supreme among the nations, supreme
   on the earth!'

SILENT PRAYER

Forgive us our sins of insolent pride.
Help us to be still in a hurried and restless world.

MEDITATION

Pictures of our planet taken in outer space show both its beauty and its fragility. We are aware that in today's world forces have been unleashed which can shake the world to its very foundations and these must be controlled if we are not to be enslaved by them. Such subjects as nuclear physics and genetic engineering present gigantic and unprecedented challenges. Human searching alone is no answer. Christ is the One who can show us the Way.

Let us intercede for scientific researchers facing complex moral issues. Help us, Lord, to appreciate that there is no other name than that of Jesus by which we can be saved.

SILENT PRAYER

It is an honour to suffer disturbing humiliations
for the sake of the name of Jesus.
Praise his holy name unceasingly.

THE WORD OF HOPE   2 Pet 3:12b-15a

The heavens will be kindled and dissolved, and the elements will melt with fire! But according to his promise we wait for new heavens and a new earth in which righteousness dwells.

Therefore, beloved, since you wait for these, be zealous to be found by him without spot or blemish, and at peace. And count the forbearance of our Lord as salvation.

'Truly this man was the Son of God!'

THE WORD IN THE GOSPEL   Mark 15:39

And when the centurion, who stood facing him saw that he thus breathed his last, he said, 'Truly this man was the Son of God!'

THE WORD IN THE PSALMS

O precious in the eye of the Lord   115:15
   is the death of his faithful.

I will declare the Lord's mighty deeds   70:16,18
   proclaiming your justice, yours alone.
Let me tell of your power to all ages,
   praise your strength and justice to the skies,
tell of you who have worked such wonders,
   O God, who is like you?

All the earth shall remember and return to
    the Lord,   21:28-30,32
   all families of the nations worship before him
for the kingdom is the Lord's; he is ruler
   of the nations.
   They shall worship him, all the mighty
   of the earth;
before him shall bow all who go down
   to the dust.
   And my soul shall live for him, my children
   serve him.
They shall tell of the Lord to generations yet to come;
   declare his faithfulness to peoples yet unborn:
'These things the Lord has done.'
   It is he, the Lord Most High,   86:5
who gives each his place.

You will not leave my soul among the dead,   15:10,11
   nor let your beloved know decay.
You will show me the path of life,

the fullness of joy in your presence,
at your right hand happiness for ever.

SILENT PRAYER

We adore you, O Christ, and we bless you because by
your holy Cross you have redeemed the world.

MEDITATION

Once scorned as merely the carpenter's son, we today
join the centurion in acknowledging Jesus as the Son of
God, and that profession of our faith constitutes our
treasure. Let us thank the Lord for the gift of faith and
the countless moments of spiritual insight. May we
lovingly behold

– the Shepherd King who laid down His life for his
sheep

– the Second Adam who restored us to life, a more
abundant life.

Lord, in the third millennium may every single
family of the nations worship before you.

Let us intercede for the Church and its leaders
throughout the world, for those preparing for baptism
and confirmation and for those who do not believe in
God, but are seeking the truth with a sincere heart.

SILENT PRAYER

When you have lifted up the Son of Man,
you will know I am he.
I draw all to myself.

THE WORD OF HOPE   1 John 4:14-16

And we have seen and testify that the Father has sent
his Son as the Saviour of the world. Whoever confesses
that Jesus is the Son of God, God abides in him, and he
in God. So we know and believe the love God has for
us. God is love, and he who abides in love abides in
God, and God abides in him.

They did not break his bones

THE WORD IN THE GOSPEL   John 19:31-33

Since it was the day of Preparation, in order to prevent
the bodies from remaining on the cross on the sabbath
(for that sabbath was a high day) the Jews asked Pilate
that their legs might be broken, and that they might be
taken away. So the soldiers came and broke the legs of
the first, and of the other who had been crucified with
him; but when they came to Jesus and saw that he was
already dead, they did not break his legs.

THE WORD IN THE PSALMS

How long, O Lord, will you forget me?   12:2,3
   How long will you hide your face?
How long must I bear grief in my soul,
   this sorrow in my heart day and night?
How long shall my enemy prevail?

O God, hear my prayer;   53:4
   listen to the words of my mouth,
for I am poor and needy,   108:22
   my skin clings to my bones.   101:6
You have burdened me with bitter troubles   70:20,21
   but you will give me back my life.
You will raise me from the depths of the earth;
   you will exalt and console me again.

The Lord is close to the broken-hearted;   33:19-21
   those whose spirit is crushed he will save.
Many are the trials of the just man
   but from them all the Lord will rescue him.
He will keep guard over all his bones,
   not one of his bones shall be broken.

110

SILENT PRAYER

> The Father says: I have loved you
> with an everlasting love;
> I have no wish to destroy.

MEDITATION

Freely and humbly Jesus had given himself up for us as a fragrant offering and sacrifice to His Father. May we never cease trying to follow his example, not claiming our rights, but respecting those of others. May we expend ourselves in the service of others, bearing their griefs and building up the Mystical Body of Christ. Then, we too can make our spiritual journey free from attachment to this world and become more prepared to meet the Father in the next.

Let us pray for the broken-hearted and the bereaved who cry out, 'How long must I bear this grief in my soul? How long will you hide your face?' Let us remember those whose spirit is so crushed that they are contemplating suicide.

SILENT PRAYER

> Lamb of God, show us your mercy.
> You are worthy to be given wisdom and strength.

THE WORD OF HOPE   Wis 1:13-14a,15

God did not make death,
and he does not delight in the death of the living.
For he created all things that they might exist,
and the generative forces of the world are wholesome,
and there is no destructive poison in them.
For righteousness is immortal.

His side was pierced

THE WORD IN THE GOSPEL   John 19:34-35

One of the soldiers pierced his side with a spear, and at
once there came out blood and water. He who saw it
has borne witness – his testimony is true, and he knows
that he tells the truth – that you also may believe.

THE WORD IN THE PSALMS

My heart is pierced within me.   108:22
O men, how long will your hearts be closed,   4:3
    will you love what is futile and seek
    what is false?

O children of Abraham, his servant,   104:6-10
    O sons of the Jacob he chose.
He, the Lord, is our God:
    his judgements prevail in all the earth.
He remembers his covenant for ever,
    his promise for a thousand generations,
the covenant he made with Abraham,
    the oath he swore to Isaac.
He confirmed it for Jacob as a law,
    for Israel as a covenant for ever.
O Lord, of salvation, bless your people!   3:9
Your love, O Lord, is eternal,   137:7
    discard not the work of your hands.

Do not fret because of the wicked;   36:1,2,5,7
    for they wither quickly like grass
    and fade like the green of the fields.
Commit your life to the Lord,
    trust in him and he will act.
Be still before the Lord and wait in patience.

SILENT PRAYER

Thus has it pleased him whom I love.
My beloved to me and I to him.

MEDITATION

The heart of Jesus was pierced by the sword and from it
flowed blood and water. The Church was born. Lord,
we do indeed commit our lives to you; we are subjects
of the new covenant with you as the king and centre of
our hearts. Your infinite love and compassion are
revealed, and of your fullness we have all received.

Beloved Lord, have mercy on us; crucified Christ
have mercy on us. We recommend to your mercy the
victims of AIDS and of other serious and progressive
diseases. Console and strengthen their carers. Draw all
people to yourself.

SILENT PRAYER

He was pierced through for our faults.
He redeemed us with his precious blood.

THE WORD OF HOPE   Eph 5:25b-27

Christ loved the church and gave himself up for her,
that he might sanctify her, having cleansed her by the
washing of water with the word, that he might present
the church to himself in splendour, without spot or
wrinkle or any such thing, that she might be holy and
without blemish.

Joseph laid the body in his own new tomb

THE WORD IN THE GOSPEL Matt 27:57-60a

When it was evening, there came a rich man from Arimathea, named Joseph, who was also a disciple of Jesus. He went to Pilate and asked for the body of Jesus. Then Pilate ordered it to be given to him. And Joseph took the body and wrapped it in a clean linen shroud, and laid it in his own new tomb, which he had hewn in the rock.

THE WORD IN THE PSALMS

Of old you spoke in a vision. 88:20-23,28,39,41,44,46
To your friends the prophets you said:
'I have exalted one chosen from the people,
   and with my holy oil anointed him.
My hand shall always be with him
   and my arm shall make him strong.
The enemy shall never outwit him
   nor the evil man oppress him.
And I will make him my first-born,
   the highest of the kings of the earth.
And yet . . . you have broken down all his walls
   and reduced his fortresses to ruins.
You have made his sword give way,
   you have not upheld him in battle;
you have cut short the years of his youth.

Why, O Lord, do you hold back your hand? 73:11
   Why do you keep your right hand hidden?
When will you console me? 118:82,84
   When will you judge my foes?
To you, Lord God, my eyes are turned. 140:8

In my justice I shall see your face 16:15
   and be filled, when I awake, with the sight
   of your glory.

I am sure now that the Lord   19:7
   will give victory to his anointed,
will reply from his holy heaven
   with the mighty victory of his hand.

SILENT PRAYER

Be sensitive to those in need of consolation
and practical help.
Remember that life means Christ.

MEDITATION

People continue to ask 'why' and 'when' as seemingly
hopeless situations persist. We are conscious of the
apparently interminable spiral of mindless crime and of
social problems passed from one generation to the next.
Nevertheless the victory of Christ, the anointed one, has
been won. Let us acknowledge the price he paid for our
salvation in bodily humiliation and be aware of the
apparent collapse of his supporters.

Let us pray for families and communities which are
disintegrating. May our own confidence be increased.
O Lord, you are below all things supporting them and
beyond all things enclosing them. You could not be held
indefinitely within a tomb. Our true life is bound up
with yours and hidden in yours. Apart from you we can
do nothing. You are the vine, we the branches.

SILENT PRAYER

We are part of Christ's Mystical Body.
Bring to others the gift of a listening heart.

THE WORD OF HOPE   Col 2:9,10a,12

In him (Christ) the whole fullness of deity dwells
bodily, and you have come to fullness of life in him. You
were buried with him in baptism, in which you were
also raised with him through faith in the working of
God, who raised him from the dead.

A great stone was rolled to the door of the tomb

The Word In The Gospel Matt 27:60b

He (Joseph) rolled a great stone to the door of the tomb.

The Word In The Psalms

Lord my God . . .	87:2
I cry at night before you.	
Save me in your merciful love;	6:5,6
for in death no one remembers you,	
from the grave, who can give you praise?	
You have laid me in the depths of the tomb,	87:7,9,17,19
in places that are dark, in the depths.	
Imprisoned, I cannot escape;	
your fury has swept down upon me;	
your terrors have utterly destroyed me.	
Friend and neighbour you have taken away:	
my one companion is darkness.	

But you, O Lord, know my path.	141:4
You, O Lord, are my lamp,	17:29-32
my God who lightens my darkness.	
With you I can break through any barrier.	
As for God, his ways are perfect;	
the word of the Lord, purest gold.	
He indeed is the shield	
of all who make him their refuge.	
For who is God but the Lord?	
Who is a rock but our God?	

Blessed are they who put their trust in God	2:12
Blessed be the Lord, the God of Israel	40:14
from age to age. Amen. Amen.	

SILENT PRAYER

> Blessed are they who receive grace to gaze
> into the depths.
> Your merciful love never fails.

MEDITATION

O Lord, your love fills all, even your own tomb, for you
are within all. Every single day the gift of divine love in
our hearts has to be rekindled into a blaze of
compassion; such meditation is a task which demands
our deepest concentration and gives us a joyful
purpose.

Help us, Lord, not to be full of ourselves and the
multiplicity of diversions offered by our society. May
we renounce ourselves and many legitimate pleasures
so that, empty of our false self, we may be filled with
your divine life. May we be built up as living stones
into a spiritual house and a holy priesthood to offer
spiritual sacrifices for the Church and the world. May
we yearn for everlasting life with insatiable desire.

With you we can break through any barrier.

SILENT PRAYER

> No one comes to the Father but through me.
> For all eternity you live and intercede for us.

THE WORD OF HOPE   Rom 13:11b-13a

It is full time now for you to wake from sleep. For
salvation is nearer to us now than when we first
believed; the night is far gone, the day is at hand. Let us
then cast off the works of darkness and put on the
armour of light; let us conduct ourselves becomingly as
in the day.

ACKNOWLEDGEMENTS

Gospel Texts
From the Revised Standard Version Bible,
Catholic Edition, copyright 1965 and 1966 by the
Division of Christian Education of the National Council
of the Churches of Christ in the USA.
Used by permission.

Psalms
Taken from *The Psalms: A New Translation*,
published by HarperCollins Publishers,
and used by permission of A.P. Watt Ltd
on behalf of The Grail, England.